May this book enrich your relationship

with almighty God, the loving Father

who longs to talk with you daily.

TO:

_____

FROM:

_____

DATE:

_____

JOHN MACARTHUR

LORD, TEACH ME
to
PRAY

An Invitation to Intimate Prayer

COUNTRYMAN®

Nashville, Tennessee

Acknowledgements

D. A. Carson. *A Call to Spiritual Reformation,* (Grand Rapids: Baker, 1992)

C. H. *Spurgeon's Prayers,* (New York, Chicago, Toronto, London, Edinburgh: Fleming H. Revell Company, 1906)

Published in association with the literary agency of Wolgemuth & Associates, Inc.

J. Countryman® is a trademark of Thomas Nelson Inc.

Project Editor: Kathy Baker

Designed by Deanna Pierce and Russ McIntosh,
The Office of Bill Chiaravalle, Sisters, Oregon

ISBN 1-4041-0024-5

Printed and bound in the United States of America

www.thomasnelson.com
www.jcountryman.com

TABLE OF CONTENTS

A PRAYER *of*
JOHN MACARTHUR

God, we know that You are mighty. Your power is over all Your creation. We bless You as the true and only living God, Creator, Sustainer and Consummator of the universe. We thank You that You are also a Savior.

We are grateful to our divine Redeemer, the Lord Jesus Christ. So great was His goodness in undertaking our redemption and being willing to be made sin for us to conquer all our foes! Great is His strength to endure the extremities of divine wrath, to bear the load of all our iniquities. Great is His love in manifesting Himself alive for us that all our fears might vanish, every doubt be removed and that we might have eternal life and a relationship to the only true God which is forever inseparable.

We thank You, O God, for the great grace that is ours in Christ that we might enjoy eternal rest, eternal peace, eternal joy and eternal glory even though we are unworthy, because we have been covered by the worthy One, the Lord Jesus Christ. May we live constantly repenting of sin, constantly desiring to conquer temptation and Satan, finding victory in the Spirit so that all that You have prepared for us we may enjoy in fullness. These things we ask that Jesus Christ would be glorified in us. Amen.

INTRODUCTION

I recently looked into the face of my newest grandchild (number 12!) and watched his blue eyes following my lips as I spoke to him. At seven weeks, he could only respond with a soft coo. In a few months, he'll begin to form words, and our relationship will blossom. He'll find me an eager provider of anything he needs.

All parents (and grandparents) eagerly await a baby's first words and joyfully nurture the development of vocabulary and speech, because communication is a precious and essential part of every loving relationship. Children soon learn the joy of speaking and how critical it is to having their needs and desires met. It is the same with the children of God, who desire to speak to the Father to express love and dependence. And the Father cherishes such prayers. As Proverbs 15:8 says, "the prayer of the upright is His delight."

The essence of prayer is talking to God as you would to a beloved parent. It is intimate and loving communication. The Bible encourages us that as children of the heavenly Father we can address Him as "Abba, Father." That biblical expression is a tender term of endearment, the equivalent of calling the Eternal God "Papa," or "Daddy."

Such an idea of intimacy with God was foreign to most Jewish people in Jesus' day. They had been taught by all the leading rabbis that God was far off, behind a veil in the holiest place, and thus unapproachable. When God appeared on Mount Sinai, the Israelites witnessed His presence accompanied by a frightening display of thunder, smoke, and lightning, because "God is a consuming fire" (Hebrews 12:29), not an intimate "Papa."

How can anyone have intimate access to the holy God of the universe? Yet that is precisely what we have when we go to God in prayer. And not just access, but unlimited divine resources—more than enough for our needs—freely available from a loving heavenly Father. In this book we'll encounter what it means to enter the presence of the infinitely awesome and majestic God and yet feel welcome there because He longs to have us with Him, telling Him all the issues of our hearts, casting all our cares on Him because He cares for us.

The essence of prayer is talking to God as you would to a beloved parent. It is intimate and loving communication.

Prayer is not only an intimate privilege; it is also a passion. Relatively few passages in Scripture directly command us to pray, but many passages tell us how to pray. Most of what Scripture teaches about prayer is based on the assumption that a fervent desire for prayer will arise from every believer's heart. The deepest longings of a Spirit-filled heart flow out in prayer, and expressions of this longing for communion with God are illustrated in several Scriptures.

Psalm 55:1-2, for example, says, "Give ear to my prayer, O God, and do not hide Yourself from my supplication. Attend to me, and hear me." Psalm 61:1-2 says, "Hear my cry, O God; attend to my prayer. From the end of the earth I will call to You, when my heart is overwhelmed." The psalmist was compelled to pray from the condition of his heart.

The passions of the heart will come out in prayers. If we examine what we pray for and find we are praying only for our own needs, problems, questions, and struggles, that is an indication of where our heart is. If we pray infrequently, briefly, and in a shallow manner, we need to do a spiritual inventory to see if the problem is a cold heart. A call to the duty of prayer will not overcome spiritual indifference, because prayer is an internal compulsion born out of a love for and dependence on our heavenly Father. Lack of prayer doesn't mean merely that we are disobedient; it is also an indicator that our love for God has grown cold.

I hope this book will awaken a renewed passion to pray to our great and gracious God. In many ways this is a simple primer on prayer. In chapters 1–3 we will take a look at the basics of prayer: why we should pray, what the conditions are for prayer, and when and how often we should pray. In the next three chapters we will examine what the content of prayer should be; I think you'll be surprised by some of what Scripture teaches on the subject. Then we'll discover some of the sins that will hinder our prayers and how to overcome those sins. In conclusion, we will look at ten incentives that motivate my own prayers.

It is my prayer for you that *Lord, Teach Us to Pray* will rekindle the fire of your passion for prayer and your love for the heavenly Father, so that you will enjoy the intimate access you have to the throne of grace and the resultant blessings He provides those who ask according to His will.

I wouldn't want to live life without "an invisible means of support." And I don't have to. Neither does anyone who is a child of God.

The eternal Creator, Sustainer, Lord, Redeemer, and loving Father of His children is that invisible power supplying us supernaturally.

Lack of prayer doesn't mean merely that we are disobedient; it is also an indicator that our love for God has grown cold.

All the infinitely rich and inexhaustible resources of heaven are available for us as God responds to our prayers. We are blessed with a boundless treasury of all spiritual blessings in Christ Jesus—some received already; others waiting to be delivered. The access to the riches of God's grace is only by means of prayer. "You do not have because you do not ask" (James 4:2).

The psalmist said, "The LORD is near to all who call upon Him" (Psalm 145:18). The confidence of David, even under the threat of death from his enemy, can be our confidence. He wrote, "In my distress I called upon the LORD, and cried out to my God; He heard my voice from His temple, And my cry came before Him, even to His ears" (Psalm 18:6). The generous promise of God Himself is: "Call upon Me in the day of trouble; I will deliver you, and you shall glorify Me" (Psalm 50:15).

A fitting response to this gracious intent on God's part is expressed in Psalm 116:1-2: "I love the LORD, because He has heard My voice and my supplications. Because He has inclined His ear to me, therefore I will call upon Him as long as I live."

Our Lord Jesus reiterated the commitment of God to hear the prayers of His children when He promised: "Ask, and it will be given to you; seek, and you will find; knock, and it will be opened to you. For everyone who asks receives, and he who seeks finds, and to him who knocks it will be opened" (Matthew 7:7-8).

The Holy Spirit through Paul encouraged us all by writing, "Be anxious for nothing, but in everything by prayer and supplication, with thanksgiving, let your requests be made known to God" (Philippians 4:6). Paul did just that through all the suffering and persecution he endured. He was able to endure seemingly unbearable amounts of pain and mistreatment, torment and abuse—because He had learned to cast all His care on the Lord in prayer (1 Peter 5:7). And he concluded from his own vast experience, "My God shall supply all your need according to His riches in glory by Christ Jesus" (Philippians 4:19).

The passions of the heart will come out in prayers.

The beloved apostle John summed up perhaps the most important prayer-principle of all when he wrote: "Now this is the confidence that we have in Him, that if we ask *anything according to His will,* He hears us. And if we know that He hears us, whatever we ask, we know that we have the petitions that we have asked of Him" (1 John 5:14-15, emphasis added). When our desires and requests are first aligned with and subjugated to the will of God, we know that He will hear and grant what we seek of Him.

How do we align our praying with the will of God? By getting to know the Scriptures. That is where God's will is revealed. Let the truth of Scripture shape your thinking and feed your appetites, and then you will know how to pray according to the will of God.

Finally, we also read in 1 John 3:22, "Whatever we ask we receive from Him, because we keep His commandments and do those things that are pleasing in His sight." Prayer must come from an obedient heart. Those who spurn God's authority in their lives should not imagine that by reciting mere words they can elicit blessings from God. Proverbs 28:9 says, "One who turns away his ear from hearing the law, even his prayer is an abomination." Thus to the willfully disobedient, God says, "Though they cry in My ears with a loud voice, I will not hear them" (Ezekiel 8:18; Isaiah 1:15; Jeremiah 11:11; Jeremiah 14:12; Micah 3:4).

Yet even the most wicked and disobedient will find God eager to pardon them and answer their prayers when they have a true change of heart, repent of their disobedience, and call upon Him. "He will abundantly pardon" (Isaiah 55:7). "He will be very gracious to you at the sound of your cry; when He hears it, He will answer you" (Isaiah 30:19). God Himself says, "Call upon Me in the day of trouble; I will deliver you, and you shall glorify Me" (Psalm 50:15). It was the testimony of the psalmist: "This poor man cried out, and the LORD heard him, and saved him out of all his troubles" (Psalm 34:6).

With all these promises and assurances, "Let us therefore come boldly to the throne of grace, that we may obtain mercy and find grace to help in time of need" (Hebrews 4:16).

Clearly, the repeated message of Scripture is that prayer moves the riches of God's supernatural grace from heaven to earth—from His throne to our need. He will respond to our cries and do what is best for us in each experience of life, while still fulfilling His perfect eternal purpose for us.

All the infinitely rich and inexhaustible
resources of heaven are available for us as
God responds to our prayers.

CHAPTER ONE

WHY PRAY?

od has revealed in Scripture His limitless sovereign power. He controls all creation, and nothing is outside His control. God Himself said:

"Remember the former things of old, For I am God, and there is no other; I am God, and there is none like Me, declaring the end from the beginning, and from ancient times things that are not yet done, saying, 'My counsel shall stand, and I will do all My pleasure ... Indeed I have spoken it; I will also bring it to pass. I have purposed it; I will also do it."

— ISAIAH 46:9-11

There is a growing response among Christians today to the truth of God's sovereignty. More and more Christians are realizing that God rules absolutely, allowing and controlling everything by His will and strength. Nothing is too hard for Him (Jeremiah 32:27). Nothing escapes His notice (Matthew 10:29). Everything works according to His perfect will and plan (Ephesians 1:11). He determined His perfect purpose before the world was formed and decreed the end of all things before anything even began (Isaiah 46:10). He knows the future because He planned it. God is working through His providence in the midst of everything that occurs, making sure all things work together for His glory and for the good of those who love Him (Romans 8:28).

Because we know that God's power is invincible and His will unhindered, we should have unwavering faith in coming to His throne in prayer.

As encouraging and confidence-building as that truth is, some people might think prayer is a waste of time and energy. Because God's will cannot fail to be accomplished, and if He is in complete control of everything anyway, does that fact destroy our motivation to pray?

No, it doesn't. God has ordained the means as well as the end, and it is His design that the prayers of His people should be the means by which He is frequently moved to act. James wrote, "The effective, fervent prayer of a righteous man avails much" (James 5:16). God, who sovereignly decreed His judgment against Israel in the time of King Ahab, also ordained that the prayer of Elijah would be the effectual means through which the judgment was brought (James 5:17-18).

A strong, confident, biblical view of the sovereignty of God does not preclude prayer; rather, it should do the opposite. Because we know that God's power is invincible and His will unhindered, we should have unwavering faith in coming to His throne in prayer. Any theological perspective that holds otherwise is simply bad theology. And any view that strips believers of their passion to pray is disobedient Christianity. Our hearts cry out in prayer because the One who is absolute ruler of all things is also our loving heavenly Father. Our confidence in His sovereignty is the

very thing that gives us "boldness and access with confidence through faith in Him" (Ephesians 3:12).

The Bible details at least five reasons we ought to pray:

- PRAYER IS COMMANDED
- IT IS A SIN NOT TO PRAY
- PRAYER GIVES GLORY TO GOD
- PRAYER ALIGNS US WITH GOD'S PURPOSES
- PRAYER RESULTS IN ANSWERS

PRAYER *Is* COMMANDED

The Holy Spirit commands us to be "praying always with all prayer and supplication" (Ephesians 6:18) and to "pray without ceasing" (1 Thessalonians 5:17). This is not a mere suggestion—we don't have the option to ignore it because we can't determine how our prayer fits into God's plans. Even though we cannot know how our prayers work within God's eternal rule and purpose, we are to pray. And, remember, it is normal for believers to do so. It is that passion again. The commands only reaffirm for us that we are supposed to do what we really long to do! It is not up to us to resolve all the mysteries of the divine mind, but to engage obediently in this privileged, intimate communion.

Prayer is a duty, and the neglect
of prayer is therefore a sin.

It Is *a* Sin Not *to* Pray

Because we are commanded to pray, it is an act of disobedience if we don't pray. We see this clearly in a remarkable Old Testament account.

During the time of the prophet Samuel, the nation of Israel demanded a king. Samuel rebuked them for their presumption and reminded them that God had given them Moses when they needed a deliverer and Aaron when they needed a mediator. He also sent them judges when they needed leadership. Their demand for a king was therefore a sin, motivated only by their desire to be like all the other nations (1 Samuel 8:5).

The people then begged Samuel, "Pray for your servants to the LORD your God, that we may not die; for we have added to all our sins the evil of asking a king for ourselves" (1 Samuel 12:19).

To calm their fears, Samuel replied, "The LORD will not forsake His people, for His great name's sake, because it has pleased the LORD to make you His people" (1 Samuel 12:22). That was wonderful reassurance. God would not forsake the nation because they were crucial to His plan. God's sovereign choice of Israel was irrevocable (Romans 11:29).

But then Samuel said, "Far be it from me that I should sin against the LORD in ceasing to pray for you" (1 Samuel 12:23). He acknowledged his responsibility to pray for them (even though he already knew how God would answer his prayers) because he understood that prayer is a duty, and the neglect of prayer is therefore a sin.

PRAYER GIVES GLORY *to* GOD

God doesn't answer our prayers for our benefit only; He answers them primarily for His own pleasure and glory. During the Last Supper, Jesus made monumental promises to His disciples. One of the marvelous guarantees He gave them was, "If you ask anything in My name, I will do it" (John 14:14). That amazing promise had a reason, and it was not merely for the benefit of those who asked. Rather, Jesus said it was "that the Father may be glorified in the Son" (John 14:13).

God answers prayers so He will be glorified. Prayer isn't primarily to give us what we want. God cares whether we have what we need, and He wants us to be blessed through our petitions. And He therefore responds by pouring out blessings on those who pray. But the primary reason for all those blessings and provisions is to put God's goodness, wisdom, power, and grace on display.

For example, when we pray that God will redeem a certain person and he or she comes to Christ, what is our first response? Of course, we thank the Lord for saving that individual. Why? Because we realize that salvation comes from God, and we glorify Him as a result. But suppose we hadn't been praying for that person when he came to Christ. God still saved him, but we did not experience the joy of that salvation or give glory to God in the same personal way ... because we weren't praying. The same is true if, for example, members of a Bible study or Sunday school class have been praying for someone's illness, job prospect, or marriage relationship. The people who have been involved in heartfelt prayers have known that God answered their prayers and are able to give God glory for the display of His grace and power. Those who are uninvolved in praying are comparatively indifferent to the display of God's glory in answering prayer. If I'm not involved in the prayer process, then I'm not going to be nearly as involved in the rejoicing. Our attitude should be, "How can I get involved in praying for as much as I possibly can so that I often see God display His divine power, mercy, grace, love, and all His other attributes?"

The primary issue in prayer is not obtaining what we want but allowing God to display His glory.

While God answers prayer to glorify Himself, we must still maintain a watchful care and concern for His name and glory.

The prophet Daniel prayed specifically that God would be glorified in answering this prayer:

> "O Lord, according to all Your righteousness, I pray, let Your anger and Your fury be turned away from Your city Jerusalem, Your holy mountain; because for our sins, and for the iniquities of our fathers, Jerusalem and Your people are a reproach to all those around us. Now therefore, our God, hear the prayer of Your servant, and his supplications, and for the Lord's sake cause your face to shine on Your sanctuary, which is desolate. O my God, incline your ear and hear; open your eyes and see our desolations, and the city which is called by Your name; for we do not present our supplications before you because of our righteous deeds, but because of Your great mercies. O Lord, hear! O Lord, forgive! O Lord, listen and act! Do not delay for Your own sake, my God, for Your city and Your people are called by Your name."

DANIEL 9:16-19

The people who have been involved in heartfelt prayers have known that God answered their prayers and are able to give God glory for the display of His grace and power.
If I'm not involved in the prayer process,
then I'm not going to be nearly as involved in the rejoicing.

The nations interpreted the captivity of Judah and the destruction of the Temple in Jerusalem as indications that God was either powerless or non-existent. So Daniel prayed for God to vindicate His name and not to allow his sin or the sin of the people to slander the Sovereign's name and corrupt His reputation. That is a mature prayer. Too many people today tend to pray only for their own desires, forgetting that God is to be glorified. So pray that God will manifest Himself in your life and the lives of those you pray for so that He may be glorified in you.

In other words, the primary issue in prayer is not obtaining what we want but allowing God to display His glory. If we receive what we want, that is really just a bonus. The eternal benefit of prayer is that it magnifies God's glory. That is why we know we will receive from Him what is best for us and what glorifies Him most. Our faith in God's power will increase as we see Him work.

PRAYER ALIGNS US
with GOD'S PURPOSES

A little boy knelt beside his bed one night and prayed, "God bless Mommy, God bless Daddy," and then at the top of his voice, he yelled, "and God, I want a new bicycle!" His mom said, "God isn't deaf." He replied, "I know. But Grandma's in the next room and she's hard of hearing." His idea was that if God didn't answer his prayer, maybe Grandma would.

We don't like to admit it, but a lot of our prayers are like that. We pray with the idea that we can pull God into line with our plans. But that is not the goal of prayer. When you begin to seek God's purposes in your prayers, your heart will be aligned with His will. That's when you will really begin to see your prayers fulfilled.

When you begin to seek God's purposes in your prayers, your heart will be aligned with His will. That's when you will really begin to see your prayers fulfilled.

When Jesus taught His disciples to pray, He began:
> *"Our Father in heaven,*
> *hallowed be Your name.*
> *Your kingdom come.*
> *Your will be done*
> *on earth as it is in heaven."*

MATTHEW 6:9-10

Only after that priority did Jesus teach us to pray for our daily bread, forgiveness, and guidance away from temptation. So Jesus' model for prayer teaches us first to get in harmony with the divine purpose. Once you understand that, you won't treat God as if He were some utilitarian genie who is stuck granting your wishes because He promised you riches in Christ—and you won't view prayer quite as selfishly.

Jesus' model for prayer teaches us first to get in harmony with the divine purpose. Once you understand that, you won't treat God as if He were some utilitarian genie who is stuck granting your wishes because He promised you riches in Christ— and you won't view prayer quite as selfishly.

Here are some examples of how we line up our prayers with God's purposes. Daniel understood from Jeremiah's prophecy that the Babylonian Captivity would last seventy years (Daniel 9:2). Yet that did not stop him from asking God to restore Israel from the captivity (Daniel 9:3–19). Daniel's prayer expressed the cry of his heart for God's will to be done. Knowing that God sovereignly chose those who will be saved (Romans 9:16,18,24)—and even that He promised to save all Israel someday (Romans 11:26)—did not keep Paul from saying, "Brethren, my heart's desire and prayer to God for Israel is that they may be saved" (Romans 10:1).

In Luke 22:31 Jesus warned Peter, "Simon, Simon! Indeed, Satan has asked for you, that he may sift you as wheat." The Lord knew it was impossible for Peter to lose his salvation, yet He told him, "I have prayed for you, that your faith should not fail" (Luke 22:32). If Jesus, the sovereign God in human flesh, prayed for God's eternal plan to be realized, how can we do any less?

A final illustration comes from the last chapter of the Bible. Although the return of Jesus Christ is promised by God and is a major theme in Revelation, John still cried out, "Come, Lord Jesus" (Revelation 22:20)—and he urged us to pray the same prayer (Revelation 22:17).

PRAYER RESULTS *in* ANSWERS

Prayer not only aligns my heart with God's sovereign plan, but also is effective in bringing about His plan. God answers prayer, and that alone should be reason enough to pray. Remember, James 5:16 clearly states, "The effective, fervent prayer of a righteous man avails much." This truth is parallel to God's electing a person to salvation, but using another's faithful witness to bring about that salvation. God, who ordained the ends, nonetheless commands us to employ the means He has chosen.

God sovereignly uses our prayers to fulfill His perfect plan. Therefore, our petitions should reflect our heart's desires.

A striking demonstration of the interaction between prayer and God's sovereignty comes from the life of godly King Hezekiah of Judah. The story is recorded in 2 Kings 20. After being informed by Isaiah the prophet that he would die from his illness, Hezekiah pleaded with God to spare his life, and God granted the king fifteen more years. Although it was not necessarily beneficial to the king, God fit it perfectly into His purpose. That incident demonstrates that a proper understanding of God's sovereignty should not lead to passive resignation but to active petition. God may choose to hear us and to change the course of events, but without altering His sovereign purpose.

The amazing, incomprehensible reality of such providence is that it is God's will all along, and our prayers are part of it.

So God sovereignly uses our prayers to fulfill His perfect plan. Therefore, our petitions should reflect our heart's desires. At the same time, we show our willingness to surrender our will to God's own holy purposes.

The Word of God actually promises: "If we know that He hears us, whatever we ask, we know that we have the petitions that we have asked of Him" (1 John 5:15). God promises to grant us what we pray for as part of His plan.

A PRAYER of
CHARLES SPURGEON

Our Father, Thy children who know Thee delight themselves in Thy presence. We are never happier than when we are near Thee. We have found a little heaven in prayer. It has eased our load to tell Thee of its weight; it has relieved our wound to tell Thee of its smart; it has restored our spirit to confess to Thee its wanderings. No place like the mercy seat for us.

We thank Thee, Lord, that we have not only found benefit in prayer, but in the answers to it we have been greatly enriched. Thou hast opened Thy hid treasures to the voice of prayer; Thou hast supplied our necessities as soon as ever we have cried unto Thee; yea, we have found it true: "Before they call I will answer, and while they are yet speaking I will hear" (Isaiah 65:24, KJV).

We do bless Thee, Lord, for instituting the blessed ordinance of prayer. What could we do without it, and we take great shame to ourselves that we should use it so little. We pray that we may be men of prayer, taken up with it, that it may take us up and bear us as on its wings towards heaven.

A Prayer *of* John MacArthur

Our Father, we understand the cry of the psalmist when he finds himself near death and asks that You would deliver him, for how can he praise You and how can he proclaim Your truth if he is in the grave? He understood how important it is that the saints praise You, that sinners may see and hear and believe and be converted. We thank You that You deliver us, You give us life so that our glory, all our powers, may sing praise to You and not be silent.

God, You are our exceeding joy and singing Your praises lifts our hearts. You are the fountain of our delight that blesses our souls to joy in You. Even as we say that, we know because of our hearts' rebellion that we do not always praise You as we should. Yet we rest ourselves in Your excellence and Your goodness and Your glory and Your loving kindness, and we find in Jesus the perfect object of inexpressible joy. We take exceeding pleasure in every thought of You, and it comes out in the sheer joy of worship.

We also know, Lord, that sometimes we are the enemy of our own worship as our sinful nature revolts and wanders from You. Although You have renewed us and changed us and justified us and are sanctifying us, there is still corruption in us that urges us away from worship, in fact to worshiping ourselves and our own desires and longings.

Bring us back, Lord, first of all to self-examination, to ask ourselves whether we are truly born again, whether our attitude is the attitude of a true child of God, whether our griefs are those of true repentance, whether our joys are the joys of genuine faith, whether our confidence in Christ is demonstrated by the work of love and the longing for what is pure and bring us to entire heart submission.

May we rejoice that You have put Your love around us from which we can never be severed, that the Savior's wounds have accomplished our redemption so that we are loved with an everlasting and eternal love that cannot be altered and nothing shall ever separate us from it. Give us life and breath that we then may, like the psalmist, praise You and proclaim Your truth to those who need so much to hear. For this privilege we would thank You in the Savior's name. Amen.

CHAPTER TWO

HOW SHOULD
WE PRAY?

 here are many ways to pray—pray on your knees, pray with your hands up, pray with your hands folded, read a prayer out of a book, pray aloud, pray silently, or pray in many other ways.

But Paul says we are to be "praying always with all prayer and supplication" (Ephesians 6:18). If we are going to be praying all the time, we must be able to pray in all kinds of different ways, because we cannot be in a special prayer-posture all day. We can pray in public or private, with loud cries, quiet whispers, or even silent thoughts. Prayer can be deliberate or spontaneous. We can be kneeling, standing, lifting up our hands, or lying prostrate. Because we are to be praying all the time, prayer must be part of the flow of our lives, and therefore it must occur in every posture.

When is the best time to pray? I attended a conference one time where a man preached on the subject of morning prayer. He quoted Psalm 63:1, which says, "Early will I seek You." He continued to look up passages that supported his point. As he did so, I kept thinking of verses that discuss praying in the evening, at noon, and during other parts of the day. He had a good point: we are to pray in the morning—but that doesn't exclude prayer in other parts of the day. Psalm 55:17 says, "Evening and morning and at noon I will pray." Daniel prayed three times a day (Daniel 6:10). Luke 6:12 says that Jesus "continued all night in prayer to God." Prayer ought to characterize our whole way of life.

There also are no set formulas for prayer. Some people think that because Jesus answered the disciples' question about how to pray by speaking the Lord's Prayer in Matthew 6:9-13, it is the only prayer Christians ever need to pray. Some believe that all prayers should begin, "Our Father, who art in heaven" (Matthew 6:9, KJV). Others believe all our prayers should conclude with a recitation of the Lord's Prayer. That is not what Jesus was teaching. He was simply providing a pattern for prayer—an outline to build on. Start praying for God's glory, then pray for your needs—bread, forgiveness, and guidance away from evil.

Prayer is not a magical incantation. Nothing in the actual words we say or how we say them can make God respond the way we want Him to—as if rote prayers repeated like a mantra or an abracadabra could move God. They actually do the opposite, as Jesus said when He rebuked the Pharisees for the "vain repetitions" in their prayers (Matthew 6:7). I do believe, however, that there are certain conditions for answered prayers. These are not rigid formulas; they are guiding principles.

- *Ask in Christ's name*
- *Ask in faith*
- *Ask in the Spirit*
- *Ask from a pure heart*

During the Last Supper, Jesus told the disciples He would be leaving, which greatly distressed them. He reassured them by saying, "If I go and prepare a place for you, I will come again and receive you to Myself" (John 14:3). The disciples had relied on Jesus for so long that they feared being without Him. He had provided all their resources. He was their beloved Friend and their spiritual, theological, and economic Leader. He was their Master in every way. He was their future as well as their present. So they panicked at the thought of His leaving. But He left them with a tremendous promise. They need not worry—even though He was leaving, they still had infinite resources. All they had to do was ask, and He would provide for them, even if He left them physically.

But notice the condition that Jesus puts on prayer: "Whatever you ask in My name, that I will do" (John 14:13). Then He repeats it in the next verse, "If you ask anything in My name, I will do it" (John 14:14). Many well-meaning believers think they have met that condition if they simply tack on the phrase, "In Jesus' name, amen," at the end of all their prayers. But "in My name" is not a verbal formula.

To understand the meaning of praying in Jesus' name, we need to understand how the word "name" is used in the Bible. In Scripture, the name of God embodies all that He is. For example, when Moses first encountered God in the burning bush, he asked Him what His name was. God replied, "I AM WHO I AM" (Exodus 3:14). That means God's name stands for all that He is. So when Christ commands us to pray in His name, He wants us to pray consistent with who He is—His person, His will, and His purposes.

So how do we know the will of Christ? Scripture gives us "the mind of Christ" in a very large measure (1 Corinthians 2:16), so we know much about what He desires. But the fact is, many times we don't know His specific will on an issue. At that point we simply need to ask God for His will to be done (Matthew 6:10). And it is always His will to bring glory to Himself.

To pray in Jesus' name therefore places limitations on how we can pray. For example, I cannot know for sure if it is God's will for a sick friend to be immediately healed. I can always confidently say, "God, I pray that he may be comforted, grow spiritually, and honor You in the midst of his trial. This I ask because I know it to be the will of Christ." That request is consistent with who Christ is and what Scripture reveals about His will. But when we pray for healing, or for the removal of a trial—or for anything else when we are not sure of the specific will of Christ—it is then necessary to pray, as Christ Himself prayed in the garden of Gethsemane, ". . . nevertheless, not as I will, but as You will" (Matthew 26:39).

Before you approach the Lord in prayer, examine what you are asking for. If you're praying for a new wardrobe, a new relationship, a new car, or something else just because you're tired of what you have, you're going to have a difficult time convincing the Lord that your motive is to fulfill God's will in your life and to glorify God through the answer to your prayer. Here is the type of prayer you ought to be offering God:

> *I want to be the kind of Christian You want me to be. I want to know Your power in my life. I want to be pure. I want to be used for Your kingdom's sake to the maximum of my abilities. I want You to give me opportunities to preach the gospel to others. This I ask in the name of Jesus Christ because I believe it is consistent with His person and work.*

When we truly pray in the name of Christ, we ought to be seeking to align ourselves with the will of God. So don't get in the habit of adding "in Jesus' name" to the end of your prayers with little or no thought for the reason you're doing so. Rather, realize to whom you are praying and why. You are coming to the Lord of the universe to be used by Him in the accomplishment of His will in your life.

> *If our prayers are consistent with the person and the will of Christ, He will hear and answer.*

Through the years, in my own personal prayer life, I have learned to always close my prayers with the following thought: "This I ask because I believe this is consistent with the will and person of the Lord Jesus Christ." Because that thought pervades my prayer, it allows me to filter out all unnecessary and selfish requests.

ASK *in* FAITH

At the end of a brief object lesson on faith, Jesus said to the disciples, "Whatever things you ask in prayer, believing, you will receive" (Matthew 21:22). All Christians need to approach God believing in His wisdom and power. He wants to see us trust Him. That's because when we trust God and He rewards that trust by answering our prayers, we have cause to praise and glorify His name.

God responds to His children who, like Abraham, "did not waver at the promise of God through unbelief, but was strengthened in faith, giving glory to God" (Romans 4:20).

If you don't believe God's promises, the Bible says you make Him a liar (1 John 5:10). As Christians, we dishonor God when we doubt Him. Unbelievers ought to be able to know Christians as those who live confidently because our trust in God is evident.

If you question whether you can trust God, go to Scripture and review the history of how God has answered the prayers of His people. Read the revelation of His sovereign majesty and wisdom. The Psalms will build your knowledge of God's person; the Law reveals His righteous character; and the historical books recount how He displayed His power on behalf of His people. That is the right foundation on which to build your faith. As your faith grows stronger, you can proceed with life in peace even before God answers each specific prayer, because you will believe that He is going to answer in His own time for your good and His glory.

ASK IN *the* SPIRIT

Do you often find yourself not knowing how to pray about a certain situation? We don't always know what best fits into God's plan. In those times that we simply don't know how to pray, the Holy Spirit helps out. Romans 8:26-27 says:

> *"The Spirit also helps in our weaknesses. For we do not know what we should pray for as we ought, but the Spirit Himself makes intercession for us with groanings which cannot be uttered. Now He who searches the hearts knows what the mind of the Spirit is, because He makes intercession for the saints according to the will of God."*

That is a great encouragement—the Holy Spirit is constantly praying for us. We have an intercessor in heaven—Christ; and we have an intercessor here on earth, in us—the Holy Spirit. Both pray to the Father on our behalf.

And notice how the Holy Spirit intercedes for us: "with groanings which cannot be uttered." Those yearnings on our behalf are prayer requests too deep and too intimate to be expressed in any way but by groaning. What a tremendous thought! The Holy Spirit yearns for our best, and God perfectly understands those yearnings because Spirit and Father are One.

God the Father, "who searches the hearts knows what the mind of the Spirit is, because [the Spirit] makes intercession for the saints according to the will of God." So even when we don't know how to pray, the Spirit of God is always praying on our behalf, and He is in perfect agreement with the heart of God. The Father understands and agrees with what the Spirit desires for us.

Ephesians 6:18 says we are to pray "in the Spirit." That simply means that because the Holy Spirit always prays in the will of God, we need to line ourselves up with Him. Offer prayers that are consistent with the Spirit's prayers so that you are committed only to God's will. I don't want one thing in my life that isn't in the will of God, and neither should you.

Praying in the Spirit is the same as praying in the name of Christ—praying in a manner consistent with who He is and what His will is. Learn to pray in concert with the Spirit. Make your prayers a duet with the One who intercedes for you.

But how do we do that? By walking in the fullness of the Spirit. As our lives are filled with the Spirit, as we walk in obedience to Him, and as we are constantly communing with God, the Spirit of God will govern our thoughts so that our prayers will be in harmony with Him. That is supernatural praying—when the Spirit of God pulls you into His praying patterns.

*We have an intercessor in heaven—Christ; and we have
an intercessor here on earth, in us—the Holy Spirit.
Both pray to the Father on our behalf.*

ASK *from* A PURE HEART

One final condition for prayer looks at personal holiness. James 5:16 says, "The effective, fervent prayer of a righteous man avails much." We need to ask from a pure heart for God to consider our prayers.

What is the righteousness James refers to? The Bible refers to two kinds of righteousness. The first is the declared, justifying righteousness of Christ that God imputes to believers through their faith. It is a forensic righteousness—based on a legal reckoning. In other words, it is a righteousness that exists outside of us but is credited to our account by faith (Philippians 3:9; Romans 4:5-6).

The other kind of righteousness is a personal and practical righteousness. We are commanded to live righteous lives. We have already been made perfectly right with God through Christ, as if we wore the perfect righteousness of Christ. But we still are commanded to live up to our position in Christ. James 5:16 is speaking of that practical righteousness. What James is saying is that if you expect God to answer your prayers, you must be committed to living a righteous life.

For example, Scripture says that the prayers of a husband will be hindered if he does not give due honor to his wife (1 Peter 3:7). It is right for a man to love his wife as Christ loves the church (Ephesians 5:25). This is God's will. To fail to do so makes one less than "a righteous man," so that his prayers do not avail much.

The apostle John wrote, "Whatever we ask we receive from Him, because we keep His commandments and do those things that are pleasing in His sight" (1 John 3:22). Obviously, personal holiness is a key condition for answered prayer. The psalmist wrote, "If I regard iniquity in my heart, The Lord will not hear" (Psalm 66:18). But, "The eyes of the LORD are on the righteous, and His ears are open to their cry" (Psalm 34:15).

Coming to God with a pure heart is really the capstone for praying as we should. If we are living righteously, we will approach God's throne in Christ's name, in faith, and according to God's will. If we consistently meet those conditions, our prayer life will be pleasing to Him, and He will answer in grace and power.

"Our Father, which art in heaven, hallowed be Thy name, Thy kingdom come, Thy will be done on earth as it is in heaven" (Matthew 6:9–10, KJV). We fear that we often begin our prayer with petitions for ourselves, and put our daily bread before Thy kingdom, and the pardoning of our sins before the hallowing of Thy name. We would not do so to-day, but guided by our Lord's model of prayer, we would first pray for Thy glory; and here, great God, we would adore Thee. Thou hast made us and not we ourselves. We are Thy people, and the sheep of Thy pasture. All glory be unto Thee, Jehovah, the only living and true God.

Oh! That to-day, even to-day, many hearts might be won to God. Convince men of the wrong of being alienated from God, put into their hearts sorrow for sin and dread of wrath to come, and lead and drive men to Christ! Oh! how we pray for this, the salvation of our fellow men, not so much for their sakes as for the sake of the glory of God and the rewarding of Christ for His pain.

Lord, help us to do Thy will. Take the crippled kingdom of our manhood and reign Thou over it. Let spirit and body be consecrated to God. May there be no reserves; may everything be given up to Thee. Reign forever! Pierced King, despised and nailed to a tree, sit Thou on the glorious high throne in our hearts, and may our lives prove that Thou art Lord over us; by our every thought and desire, and imagination, and word, and act, in every respect being under Thy divine control.

A Prayer of
John MacArthur

Father, we thank You for the rich presentation of the glories of our Savior, Your Son, heir of all things, creator of the world. Brighten us with Your glory, with the express image of Your person, the One who upholds all things by the Word of His power, the One who Himself purged our sins, the One who is seated at Your right hand, the One who has obtained an inheritance far better than angels that He has been exalted above all angels, all principalities, all powers.

We thank You, O God, that we know You, the true and living God, and Your Son the Lord Jesus Christ. We thank You that You are Creator and Redeemer God, author of all existence, source of all blessedness. We adore You for making us able to know You, for giving us reason and conscience; for leading us to desire You through the work of Your Holy Spirit. We praise You for the revelation of Yourself in the Scripture, in particular in the gospel. We thank You that Your heart is a dwelling place of pity and that Your thoughts are thoughts of peace toward us and patience and grace. We thank You for the vastness of Your mercy.

We thank You that You moved us to know how the guilty can be pardoned, and the unholy sanctified, and the poor made rich. We thank You that You have caused us to be born into new life in which we not only hear You but know You, we walk with You, we rejoice in You, we take You at Your Word. We find our life and joy and peace there. We thank You that You have given to us Your Holy Spirit with all His comforts and encouragements. We thank You for spiritual graces and blessings beyond which we can number. We thank You for duties which are more valuable to us in many ways than privileges, for they lay up for us eternal treasure in heaven which we will ever enjoy to Your eternal praise.

We ask that we would cherish the simplicity of knowing Christ and sincerity of character and life. We ask that You would wash our feet of the sin that has accumulated, that You would cleanse us and make us pure. Help us to be in reality before You what we are in appearance before people. Help us to be in our hearts true and faithful to You before we are in our songs. Help us to leave the world behind, set our affections on things above, have no interest in what is empty and foolish and sinful. And may we not only be receivers of grace but may we be dispensers of grace who will by the way we live demonstrate Your grace to others. May we proclaim the gospel of grace and in so doing prepare to bury evil if necessary. Make us worthy of our calling that the name of Jesus may be glorified in us and we in Him.

CHAPTER THREE

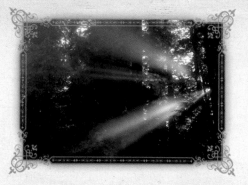

CONTINUAL,
PERSISTENT PRAYER

 great misunderstanding exists within evangelical Christianity about how often believers should pray. Many religions prescribe certain times for prayer. People in Muslim countries are summoned to prayer at set times throughout the day. Judaism prescribes certain daily hours for prayer. But some professing Christians believe that if they attend church services and participate in public prayer, then they have fulfilled their duty.

Prayer meetings and specific times for prayer are acceptable, but the Bible is quite clear that one's prayer life should not be restricted to such particulars. That is obvious from the command to "pray without ceasing" (1 Thessalonians 5:17); and "pray at all times" (Ephesians 6:18, NASB). Prayer is a way of life for true believers.

Prayer is a way of life for true believers.

Perhaps the best way to illustrate the idea of ceaseless prayer is to compare it to breathing. Inhaling and exhaling is so natural for us that it often seems totally involuntary; it's actually harder to hold your breath than it is to breathe. The same should be true of prayer for the Christian. Prayer is like breathing for us. The natural thing for us to do is commune with God. When we don't pray, we're holding our breath spiritually—fighting against the very existence and presence of God in our lives. Prayer should flow naturally and continually from our hearts.

When Paul commands us to pray without ceasing, he doesn't expect us to walk around with closed eyes all the time, nor does he mean every prayer should last an hour or more. What he does mean, however, is that we should be in constant communion with God.

I think of prayer as living in continual God-consciousness, in which everything we see and experience becomes a kind of prayer, lived in deep awareness of and surrender to our heavenly Father. Whatever happens, there is a Godward response. To obey this exhortation means that when we are tempted, we bring the temptation before God and ask for His help. When we experience something good and beautiful, we immediately thank the Lord for it. When we see evil around us, we ask God to make it right and to allow us to help remedy the evil, if such involvement is according to His will. When we meet people who do not know Christ, we pray for God to draw them to Himself and to use us as faithful witnesses. When we encounter trouble, we turn to God as our Deliverer.

Prayer is like breathing for Christians.
When you don't pray, you're holding your
breath spiritually—fighting against the very existence
and presence of God in your life.

At every waking moment you ought to be praising God or petitioning Him. Living in unbroken communion with Him makes life a continually ascending prayer. All your thoughts, deeds, and circumstances become an opportunity to commune with your heavenly Father. That's how you "set your mind on things above, not on the things on the earth" (Colossians 3:2). Or, as David said, "I have set the LORD always before me" (Psalm 16:8).

Because the ultimate purpose God has for our salvation is to glorify Himself and bring us into intimate, rich fellowship with Him, failure to seek Him in prayer is to deny that purpose. The apostle John said, "That which we have seen and heard we declare to you, that you also may have fellowship us; and truly our fellowship is with the Father and with His Son, Jesus Christ" (1 John 1:3). God's greatest desire, and our greatest need, is to be in constant fellowship with Him now, and there is no greater earthly expression or experience of that fellowship than prayer.

Living in unbroken communion with Him makes life a continually ascending prayer. All your thoughts, deeds, and circumstances become an opportunity to commune with your heavenly Father.

PERSISTENT PERSEVERANCE

Prayer is not easy. Just because we can talk to God anytime throughout the day certainly doesn't mean we will. Paul commanded the Colossians, "Continue earnestly in prayer" (Colossians 4:2), and he warned the Ephesians to be "watchful to this end with all perseverance and supplication" (Ephesians 6:18). The root word for "continue earnestly" refers to being intense. "Perseverance" means "endurance"—sticking to the task. When you pray for something, keep at it until you have an answer. To "continue earnestly in prayer" is to courageously and persistently bring everything, especially the needs of others, before God.

This matter of perseverance is taught in two parables our Lord gave. Both stories show us someone totally unlike God, yet illustrate the value of persistent prayer.

Luke 11:5-10 records one parable:

> He said to them, "Which of you shall have a friend, and go to him at midnight and say to him, 'Friend, lend me three loaves; for a friend of mine has come to see me on his journey, and I have nothing to set before him'; and he will answer from within and say, 'Do not trouble me; the door is now shut, and my children are with me in bed; I cannot rise and give to you'? I say to you, though he will not rise and give to him because he is his friend, yet because of his persistence he will rise and give him as many as he needs. So I say to you, ask, and it will be given to you; seek, and you will find; knock, and it will be opened to you. For everyone who asks receives, and he who seeks finds, and to him who knocks it will be opened."

Jesus teaches us two things about persistent prayer in that parable. First, it shows the benefits of persistence. Friendship did not benefit the man who needed the bread, but his persistence ultimately paid off because his unsympathetic friend couldn't take the irritation. But the next point Jesus makes is even more profound. If such a reluctant and sinful friend will honor persistence, how much more will our holy, loving, sympathetic heavenly Father respond to us?

A second parable also illustrates the virtue of persistence. If we don't get an immediate answer to our request, or if events don't turn out exactly or as quickly as we hoped they would, our Lord's word to us is to not lose heart (Luke 18:1). Jesus then explains why:

> "There was in a certain city a judge who did not fear God nor regard man. Now there was a widow in that city; and she came to him, saying, 'Get justice for me from my adversary.' And he would not for a while, but afterward he said within himself, 'Though I do not fear God nor regard man, yet because this widow troubles me I will avenge her, lest by her continual coming she weary me.'" Then the Lord said, "Hear what the unjust judge said. And shall God not avenge His own elect who cry out day and night to Him, though He bears long with them."
>
> —LUKE 18:2-5

The point of the story is obvious: God is the opposite of the unjust judge, who acted only because he was tired of the complaining woman. God longs to respond to His chosen children who are persistent in prayer—even though He often, for good reasons, makes us wait longer than we wish. So just keep praying without ceasing and don't give up. Keep knocking. Keep asking. Keep seeking.

We can never force God to do what we want against His will; but we do need to demonstrate to Him a heart of compassion and the genuineness of a concerned and caring soul.

Our legitimate concern for others should express itself in how fervently we take our requests to God. When Jacob wrestled with the Lord, he would not let go until God blessed him (Genesis 32:24-30). We need to exhibit that kind of persistence and earnestness. We can never, by our persistence, force God to do what we want against His will; but we do need to demonstrate to Him a heart of compassion and the genuineness of a concerned and caring soul.

Jesus Himself was the epitome of perseverance in prayer. Hebrews 5:7 says, "He had offered up both prayers and supplications, with vehement cries and tears to Him who was able to save Him from death." Passionate prayers offered with great intensity and agony characterized our Lord's life on earth. Although Scripture does not chronicle the details of His prayers, we can be sure that He persevered in them, many times all night (Luke 6:12).

The greatest illustration of His intensity in prayer took place in the garden prior to His death. Luke writes, "He knelt down and prayed, saying, 'Father, if it is Your will, take this cup away from Me; nevertheless not My will, but Yours, be done.' . . . And being in agony, He prayed more earnestly. Then His sweat became like great drops of blood falling down to the ground" (Luke 22:41-44). Another recording of this same event indicates that Jesus petitioned God three times (Matthew 26:36-46).

Our Lord performed many mighty works when He was on earth, yet in none of them is there any apparent expenditure of energy. Only when He prayed do we see Him agonize and toil over His petitions.

Our Lord performed many mighty works when He was on earth, yet in none of them is there any apparent expenditure of energy. Although Scripture says power went out of Him (Mark 5:30; Luke 8:46), there is no record that would indicate He had to exert any effort to perform His miracles. Only when He prayed do we see Him agonize and toil over His petitions, even to the point of sweating great drops of blood. Such persistence is foreign to us, yet it is that very intensity Christ wanted the disciples to learn from those two parables.

CONSTANT ALERTNESS

If we are to persevere in prayer, we must also be on the alert to situations that need our prayers. Paul says we are to "Continue earnestly in prayer" (Colossians 4:2) and that we need to be "watchful to this end" (Ephesians 6:18). Several times Jesus told the disciples to "watch and pray" (Matthew 26:41; Mark 13:33; Mark 14:38; Luke 21:36). We cannot pray intelligently unless we are alert to what is going on around us. Many Christians forget or ignore Peter's plea to be "serious and watchful in your prayers" (1 Peter 4:7). We need to keep our eyes open—to be alert to the spiritual needs of others. As we become sensitive to what is happening around us, we learn what to pray.

What is going on in the lives of the people you know? We are to be looking outward, not inward. When someone shares a need, do you really pray or do you merely say, "I'll be praying for you!"—and then forget? It is all too easy to ask others to pray for our needs, but we also need to be faithful to pray for others and watch out for their spiritual needs.

Christians sometimes pray vague, general prayers from which clear answers can't be discerned because the prayers don't express anything specific. General requests can be appropriate in certain instances, but through God's answers to specific prayers we clearly see Him put His love and power on display.

If we are not alert to the specific problems and needs of others, we can't pray about them specifically and earnestly. But when we do, we can watch for God's answer, rejoice in it when it comes, and then offer Him our thankful praise.

As we become sensitive to what is happening around us,
we learn what to pray.

A PRAYER *of* JOHN MACARTHUR

Our sovereign Lord, we praise You continually for permission to approach Your throne of grace and to spread before You our wants and our desires. We are not worthy of Your blessings, we are not worthy of Your mercies. We have no righteousness of our own. All we can ask is that You not remember our sins but that You remember mercy toward us.

And still we act in disobedience and rebellion, we experience discontent, pride, envy, anger. We fail to make the most of our spiritual opportunities and talents and gifts. We abuse Your mercy and Your grace. We waste the privilege of worship. We pervert the seasons of grace. We neglect the matters of sanctification. We treat the Scripture lightly. And most of all, we fail to love as we should the very Friend of sinners upon whom we depend for our salvation.

So we confess our guilt. We acknowledge our self-despair. Yet we remember there's hope in You because the Lamb has taken away our sin. We thank You that we have been drawn to Him, to hear Him, to trust in Him, to delight in Him, and to delight in Your Word and Your law.

Preserve our minds from error. Preserve our hearts from the love of idols. Preserve our lips from speaking deceitfully. Preserve our behavior from stain of sin, our character from any appearance of evil, and may we live as harmless, blameless children of God without rebuke in the world, holding forth the Word of Life that others may see Christ in us and be drawn to Him. These things we ask for His glory and in His name.

CHAPTER FOUR

CONFESSION

e have looked at the reasons Christians pray, the conditions for prayer, and the attitude we ought to have as we pray. Now we need to look in practical terms at how we ought to pray.

Without doubt the most important element in prayer is confession of sin.

Although many support groups encourage members to confess to their weaknesses, the church is probably the only organization where people meet together regularly to confess their problems specifically with sin itself. All Christians who take honest spiritual inventories are cognizant of personal sin. We know God hates sin and thus we are unnerved over our own iniquities. So Christians continually confess their sin. The apostle John said, "If we confess our sins, He is faithful and righteous to forgive us our sins and to cleanse us from all unrighteousness" (1 John 1:9). The original Greek words express continual confession as an essential characteristic of true holiness. The forgiveness and cleansing are also continual. As the Christian continually confesses, God continually grants pardon and purification.

As the Christian continually confesses,
God continually grants pardon and purification.

Remember, if you are justified in Christ, God has forgiven all your sins already. When Jesus Christ died on the cross, He bore the penalty for all the sins of all believers for all time—our past sins, present sins, and future sins. That's where God's complete forgiveness of the believer's sin was assured. Christians are freed from the guilt of our sins and are clothed in the perfect righteousness of Christ. Our justification before God is an accomplished fact.

If justification takes care of past, present, and future sin, so that there is no condemnation for those who are in Christ (Romans 8:1), why does Scripture plainly teach redeemed people to pray regularly for forgiveness?

The answer is that there are two aspects of forgiveness. The *judicial forgiveness* of justification makes us right with God as our judge. It is what guarantees we will never face eternal condemnation for our sins (John 5:24). But the daily forgiveness Jesus taught us to pray for is a *familial forgiveness*. It is the remedy for God's fatherly displeasure when we sin (Hebrews 12:5-11).

As long as we live in a sinful world, with our own sinful tendencies, Christians still need daily cleansing from the defiling influence of our sin.

The forgiveness we seek in our daily walk is not pardon from an angry Judge, but mercy from a grieved Father.

How this daily cleansing works is best illustrated by Peter's encounter with Jesus just prior to the Last Supper. Jesus took on the role of a servant to wash the disciples' feet, but Peter was reluctant to have Christ serve him in such a humiliating manner:

> *Peter said to Him, "You shall never wash my feet!" Jesus answered him, "If I do not wash you, you have no part with Me." Simon Peter said to Him, "Lord, not my feet only, but also my hands and my head." Jesus said to him, "He who is bathed needs only to wash his feet, but is completely clean."*
>
> —JOHN 13:8-10

Bathing illustrates the forgiveness of justification—judicial pardon. Those who are justified are forgiven the penalty of sin forever. They do not need to be justified again. The day-to-day defilement of sin still needs to be dealt with, however. God's children need His fatherly forgiveness when they dishonor Him. Sin needs to be forsaken regularly, and the pardon of a loving but displeased Father must be sought. A disobedient child is permanently the child of his father, but the relationship will not be right until the child seeks the forgiveness that restores the relationship.

When David sinned with Bathsheba, he came under such conviction that he confessed to God: "I acknowledge my transgressions, and my sin is always before me. Against You, You only, have I sinned, and done this evil in Your sight" (Psalm 51:3-4). Then he pleaded, "Restore to me the joy of

Your salvation" (Psalm 51:12). Notice that David did not ask for his salvation to be restored, but merely the joy of it.

So, again, the forgiveness we seek in our daily walk is not pardon from an angry Judge, but mercy from a grieved Father.

When we enter God's presence, we must come acknowledging that we are sinners who deserve judgment.

As David's prayer indicates, true confession of sin is not just admitting you did something wrong, but acknowledging that your sin was against God and in defiance of Him personally. So the primary feature of confession is agreeing with God that we are helplessly guilty. In fact, the Greek word for confession is *homologeo,* which literally means, "say the same." To confess our sins is to say the same thing as God says about them. Confessing our sins therefore means acknowledging that God's perspective of our transgressions is correct.

For that reason, true confession also involves a penitent attitude—turning away from the evil thought or action. You have not honestly confessed your sins until you have longed to be rid of them. Thus real confession includes a brokenness that inevitably leads to a change of behavior.

A MODEL of CONFESSION

Daniel the Old Testament prophet was a righteous, uncompromising man of God who lived a pure life in the midst of a pagan society. Yet Daniel always dealt with sin whenever he went before the Lord. When he wasn't confessing his own sin, he confessed the sin of those around him.

Before he began to pray, Daniel set his "face toward the Lord God to make request by prayer and supplications, with fasting, sackcloth, and ashes" (Daniel 9:3). When we enter God's presence, we must come acknowledging that we are sinners who deserve judgment.

Daniel begins his confession this way:

> "O Lord, great and awesome God, who keeps His covenant and mercy with those who love Him, and with those who keep His commandments, we have sinned and committed iniquity, we have done wickedly and rebelled, even by departing from Your precepts and judgments. Neither have we heeded Your servants the prophets."
>
> — DANIEL 9:4-6

Daniel sticks to this pattern for most of his prayer. Then in verse 16 he says, "O Lord, according to all Your righteousness, I pray, let Your anger and Your fury be turned away." When believers enter God's presence, it is only through His grace and mercy that any survive the encounter. Lamentations 3:22 reminds us, "[It is] through the LORD's mercies [that] we are not consumed."

THE PURPOSE *of* CONFESSION

Confession is a healthy beginning for prayer because it provides a reminder that we do not deserve anything God gives us. A materialistic perspective on prayer gets eliminated when we go before God with the brokenness and the contrite heart of people who confess their sins. When we affirm with God that we deserve nothing, we end any self-centeredness in our prayers.

Some Christians believe you should demand with authority whatever you want from God—that in fact He has obligated Himself to give them to you. But Scripture teaches we must have just the opposite attitude. In Isaiah 66:2 the Lord says, "On this one will I look: on him who is poor and of a contrite spirit, and who trembles at My word." So when you pray, go to God trembling at your own sinfulness, confessing your weaknesses and failures, and acknowledging that you deserve nothing. We are needy and dependent, as well as undeserving and sinful. We pray for answers—but only by grace.

A second reason for confessing sin is this: When any believer confesses his sin, God can chasten (discipline) him without being thought of as unfair. If He chastens us because of our sin, we know we deserve the correction.

During the conquering of Jericho, God commanded the people not to take from the spoils of the city. But a man named Achan did so (Joshua 6-7). Joshua confronted him and said, "Give glory to the Lord God of Israel, and make confession to Him"

(Joshua 7:19). Achan knew that he and his family would be destroyed for their disobedience, but Joshua wanted Achan to confess his sin so God would be exonerated from any accusation of harshness for dealing out righteous judgment.

When God chastens His children, it is for our benefit. Hebrews 12:5-11 says He chastens us as sons so that we might be better sons. Too often believers wonder why God would bring discipline on them, but confession allows us to view chastening from God's perspective. When we confess, we affirm that God's hand of heaviness on us is righteous, and we can glorify His holiness even in our trouble.

THE ELEMENTS *of* CONFESSION

As we noted earlier, David committed a terrible sin at the height of his power as king of Israel. It was a sin for which he would suffer severe consequences the rest of his life. He became infatuated with Bathsheba, the wife of one of his military officers. What began with a glance on a rooftop one day led him to lust for her and to consummate an adulterous relationship that resulted in her pregnancy. In an attempt to cover his sin, David arranged for her husband, Uriah, to lead a suicide squad into battle, then abandoned him and exposed him to a violent death. David then hypocritically gave Uriah a military funeral and married his pregnant wife (2 Samuel 11).

Through his actions, David had broken at least four of the Ten Commandments. He had coveted, stolen, committed adultery, and murdered. Guilt finally caught up with David, and he became oppressed by his sin. Psalm 51 records his outpouring of confession. There he expressed four requests:

- *Sin had made him dirty, and he asked to be cleansed.*
- *Remorse had made him sick, and he asked to be healed.*
- *Iniquity had made him sad, and he asked to be joyful.*
- *He was guilty of directly violating God's love and laws, so he asked for pardon and mercy.*

David's confession of sin in Psalm 51 shows us three crucial elements of true confession:

- *A right view of sin*
- *A right view of God*
- *A right view of self.*

A RIGHT VIEW of SIN

First, a right view of sin is the recognition that sin deserves judgment. David prayed, "Have mercy upon me, O God, according to Your lovingkindness; according to the multitude of Your tender mercies, blot out my transgressions" (Psalm 51:1). Such a plea for God's mercy was David's admission that he was guilty and unworthy of exoneration and acquittal. The possibility of mercy comes only after a guilty verdict has been rendered. In true confession, we must recognize that we do not deserve to be forgiven. The only recourse we have is to appeal to God's grace and mercy.

When we take personal responsibility for our sin,
we will advance toward spiritual maturity.

A right view of sin also recognizes an urgent need for cleansing. David prayed, "Wash me thoroughly from my iniquity, and cleanse me from my sin" (Psalm 51:2). He wanted every dirty sin removed from his life. Sin leaves a deep stain, and only a total cleansing will suffice. Just as Christ stooped to wash the disciples' feet, we need to allow Him to cleanse us from the dirt of the world every day.

Another crucial part to having a right view of sin is accepting full responsibility for it. David said, "I acknowledge my transgressions, and my sin is always before me. Against You, You only, have I sinned, and done this evil in Your sight—that You may be found just when

You speak, and blameless when You judge" (Psalm 51:3-4). David did not blame anyone but himself. Thus he honored God's chastening and did not try to escape any accountability. When we take personal responsibility for our sin, we will advance toward spiritual maturity.

A right view of sin also recognizes that we sin because it is in our nature to do so. Sin is not an anomaly, nor could we stop sinning even if we wanted to. We are sinful at the very core of our humanity. David said, "Behold, I was brought forth in iniquity, and in sin my mother conceived me" (Psalm 51:5). Sin is passed on from generation to generation at the time of conception. All of us are born utterly depraved—not necessarily as bad as we could possibly be, but nevertheless sinful in every aspect of our nature. We cannot help it; it is part of our humanity, handed down from Adam. Knowing "we were born this way, as sinners" does not exonerate us for our guilt; we still deserve condemnation. We receive forgiveness only by grace.

A RIGHT VIEW of GOD

True confession demands an accurate understanding of God. First, David recognized God's *holiness*: "You desire truth in the inward parts" (Psalm 51:6). God is not concerned with external behavior but with the thoughts and motives of our hearts.

David also referred to God's *authority over sin*: "Purge me with hyssop, and I shall be clean; wash me, and I shall be whiter than snow" (Psalm 51:7). David was confident that God would do a thorough job of cleansing him from sin. God can and will change your sinful habits, but He requires your trust in His authority over the powers of evil.

David also recognized God's *compassion*: "Make me hear joy and gladness, that the bones You have broken may rejoice". (Psalm 51:8). David had been a shepherd, and he knew that sometimes shepherds would have to break a leg of a wayward lamb to keep him from straying from the flock. Until the limb heals, the shepherd has to carry the lamb. Once he has healed, the lamb will usually follow the shepherd wherever he goes.

Finally, David understood God's *mercy*: "Hide Your face from my sins, and blot out all my iniquities" (Psalm 51:9). He knew God has the power and desire to pardon sin in those who exhibit genuine repentance.

David understood that he needed to turn from his sin and live a godly life for three reasons:

- *For the sake of sinners*
- *To glorify God*
- *For the sake of saints*

First, David knew he had to live a holy life if he was to be used by God to convert sinners to Him: "Then I will teach transgressors Your ways, and sinners shall be converted to You" (Psalm 51:13). Someone harboring personal guilt has nothing to say to others looking for relief from their sin.

Second, we are to live godly lives for the sake of God Himself: He delights in "a broken and a contrite heart" (Psalm 51:17). You bring glory to God by being sensitive to the sin in your life and then being broken before the Lord over it.

Third, we must be holy for the sake of the saints:

> *Do good in Your pleasure to Zion; build the walls of Jerusalem. Then You shall be pleased with the sacrifices of righteousness, with burnt offering and whole burnt offering; then they shall offer bulls on Your altar.*
>
> — PSALM 51:18-19

Only when we are in a right relationship with God can we intercede for others. True confession can occur only when we see God for who He is, when we see sin for what it is, and when we see ourselves for what we really are.

A PRAYER *of*
CHARLES SPURGEON

O God! we would not speak to Thee as from a distance, nor stand like trembling Israel under the law at a distance from the burning mount, for we have not come unto Mount Sinai, but unto Mount Sion, and that is a place for holy joy and thankfulness, and not for terror and bondage. Blessed be Thy name, O Lord! We have learnt to call Thee "Our Father, which art in heaven" (Matthew 6:9, KJV); so there is reverence, for Thou art in heaven; but there is sweet familiarity, for Thou art our Father.

We would draw very near to Thee now through Jesus Christ the Mediator, and we would make bold to speak to Thee as a man speaketh with his friend, for hast Thou not said by Thy Spirit, "Let us therefore come boldly unto the throne of grace" (Hebrews 4:16, KJV). We might well start away and flee from Thy face if we only remembered our sinfulness. Lord! we do remember it with shame and sorrow; we are grieved to think we should have offended Thee, should have neglected so long Thy sweet love and tender mercy; but we have now returned unto the "shepherd and bishop of [our] souls" (1 Peter 2:25, KJV). Led by such grace, we look to Him whom we crucified, and we have mourned for Him and then have mourned for our sin.

Now, Lord, we confess our guilt before Thee with tenderness of heart, and we pray Thee seal home to every believer that full and free, that perfect and irreversible charter of forgiveness which Thou gavest to all them that put their trust in Jesus Christ. Lord! Thou hast said it: "If we confess our sins, Thou art merciful and just to forgive us our sins and to save us from all unrighteousness" (1 John 1:9, KJV). There is the sin confessed: there is the ransom accepted: we therefore know we have peace with God, and we bless that glorious one who hath come "to finish transgression, and to make an end of sins" (Daniel 9:24, KJV), to bring in everlasting righteousness, which righteousness by faith we take unto ourselves and Thou dost impute unto us.

A PRAYER *of* JOHN MACARTHUR

Father, we are blessed who confess, because the promise is that if we confess, You are faithful and just to forgive us our sins. It does us no good to keep silent, to be impenitent. It dries us up. It leaves Your heavy hand of chastening on us. May we ascend Your hill with clean hands and a pure heart. May we acknowledge our sin to You and not hide our iniquity—we confess and receive Your gracious forgiveness that blesses.

Father of the Lord Jesus, help us to approach You with deepest reverence, not with presumption, and not in servile fear but with holy boldness. You are beyond the grasp of our understanding but not beyond our love. And You know that we confess to love You supremely for You are supremely wondrous, good, perfect, and glorious. Our hearts melt at the love of Jesus, our brother and our Savior, our Lord and our friend, our eternal bridegroom, dead for us, alive for us. We are overwhelmed that He is ours and we are His. He has given for us and given to us. And we thank You for the gift of Christ, and we offer in response our worship.

We confess and profess our love, but we admit that our love is often cold. Bear us away on Your great love. Make us fruitful in living in response to that love, conform our character to the beauty of the one who loves, even Jesus Christ in whose name we pray.

CHAPTER FIVE

PRAISE

fter confession, praise ought to be the next most important part of prayer. Christians cannot grow unless their lives are characterized by praise. Psalm 50:23 says, "Whoever offers praise glorifies Me." If you want to glorify God, praise Him. Proud people don't praise God—they are too consumed with themselves. But humble people are in awe of Him, and praise pours from their hearts.

Praise is so much a part of God's pattern for His people that He provided a hymnbook filled with powerful praise. The psalms are hymns that were sung by the people of Israel.

David wrote many of the psalms, and in Psalm 86 he said, "All nations whom You have made shall come and worship before You, O Lord, and shall glorify Your name. For You are great, and do wondrous things; You alone are God . . . I will praise You, O Lord my God, with all my heart, and I will glorify Your name forevermore" (Psalm 86:9-10, 12). Praising God gives Him glory.

In Psalm 92:1-2 the psalmist said, "It is good to give thanks to the LORD, and to sing praises to Your name, O Most High; to declare Your lovingkindness in the morning, and Your faithfulness every night." When you praise the Lord as you wake up, you set the tone for the day. And when you praise Him at night, you establish the pattern of praise in all of life. That should set you up to start the pattern all over again the next morning.

What does it mean to praise God? Some think you should simply shout out praises like, "Hallelujah! Praise the Lord!" Some think you should wave your hands in the air, while others think you should bow humbly and express praise silently. But as we have already learned in this book, God is not so concerned about the manner of our praise as He is the content of it. According to the Bible, praise involves three elements:

- *Naming God's attributes*
- *Naming God's works*
- *Offering thanks*

Naming God's Attributes

Scripture powerfully and extensively reveals the character of God, enabling us to praise Him better. The prophet Habakkuk, for example, revealed God's nature as eternal and holy. He wrote:

> Are You not from everlasting, O LORD my God, my Holy One? We shall not die. O LORD, You have appointed them for judgment; O Rock, You have marked them for correction. You are of purer eyes than to behold evil, and cannot look on wickedness.
>
> — HABAKKUK 1:12-13

Habakkuk also praised God for being almighty and for keeping His promises.

That praise solved a great problem for the prophet. He didn't understand why God was going to judge Israel by sending the evil Chaldeans to conquer them (Habakkuk 1:6-11). He wanted God to revive and restore His people, but they had overstepped the limit of God's patience.

In the midst of his confusion, Habakkuk remembered that God is holy—He doesn't make mistakes. God keeps His covenant—He doesn't break His promises. And he remembered that God is eternal—He is outside the flux and boundaries of history. Following those remembrances, Habakkuk said, "The just shall live by his faith" (Habakkuk 2:4). He felt better even though his circumstances hadn't changed. God did allow the Chaldeans to overrun Israel for a time, but Habakkuk knew God was wise enough and strong enough to handle anything He allowed.

Habakkuk's faith provides a powerful example for us. Instead of worrying about problems we can't solve, we should pray: "Lord, You are bigger than history. You own everything in the entire universe. You can do anything You want to do. You love me and promise that I will never be without the things I need. You said You would take care of me as You take care of the grass of the field. You have promised that Your character and power are at my disposal." That kind of praise glorifies God.

It is a good habit just to review God's character when you pray and remember that He is a God of infinite love, glory, grace, majesty, mercy, and wisdom. He is invincible!

Naming God's Works

God's attributes are manifest in His works. The psalms are filled with the record of the great things God has done. They praise Him for parting the Red Sea, bringing the people of Israel out of Egypt, opening the Jordan River, making water flow from a rock, feeding the people with manna in the wilderness, destroying Israel's enemies, making the walls of Jericho fall, and many other powerful displays.

But let's go back to Habakkuk. After reevaluating his problem, the prophet began to praise God for His works and tremble at the power displayed in them (Habakkuk 3:16). He said he would rejoice in the Lord even if everything crumbled around him (vv. 17–18). Why? Because God had proved Himself in the past. That's why the Old Testament contains such an extensive history of God's works—they prove Him to be powerful.

Whenever we have a problem we don't know how to solve, we should praise God for His wisdom and might, as demonstrated in biblical history. It is reassuring to praise God like this:

> "Lord, You are the God who put the stars and the planets into space. You are the God who formed the earth and separated the land from the sea. Then You made man and everything else that lives. Although man fell into sin, You planned his redemption. You are the God who carved out a nation for Yourself and preserved it through history. You are the God who performed wonder after wonder for that nation. You are the God who wrote the law on tablets of stone. You are the God who

enabled Your people to walk out of Egypt. You drowned Pharaoh's army. You are the God who came into this world in human form, and then rose from the dead."

That leaves little doubt that He can provide all we need!

When you spend time in praise, reviewing all that God is and all He did for His people in Old Testament times, what Christ accomplished for sinners, what God did through the disciples in the first century, and what He has done through the history of the church, your problems pale in comparison to the Lord's power. As we recite the many things God has done, we affirm His worthiness. Praise bolsters confidence in God because He has proven Himself trustworthy in the past. So when we praise God before bringing Him our problems, we can be confident that He will solve our troubles with wisdom and power—because it is His very nature to do so.

OFFERING THANKS

Naming the attributes and works of God easily leads to thanking Him for all He has done, is doing, and will do. At the heart of all praise is thanksgiving.

Luke 17 relates an encounter Jesus had with some lepers.

> As He entered a certain village, there met Him ten men who were lepers, who stood afar off. And they lifted their voices and said, "Jesus, Master, have mercy on us!" So when He saw them, He said to them, "Go, show yourselves to the priests." And so it was that as they went, they were cleansed."
>
> — LUKE 17:12-14

According to Mosaic law, a leper could not return to society unless a priest verified that his disease was in remission.

All ten men should have sought Jesus out to thank Him for the astounding miracle of healing. But Luke continues:

> One of them, when he saw that he was healed, returned, and with a loud voice glorified God, and fell down on his face at His feet, giving Him thanks. And he was a Samaritan.
>
> — LUKE 17:15-16

Only one of the ten, an outcast from Jewish society, glorified God by thanking Jesus.

Luke goes on to say:

> *So Jesus answered and said, "Were there not ten cleansed? But where are the nine? Were there not any found who returned to give glory to God except this foreigner?" And He said to him, "Arise, go your way. Your faith has made you well."*
>
> — LUKE 17:17-19

Though all ten were healed physically, only the thankful Samaritan was healed spiritually as well.

The apostle Paul emphasized the need for gratitude when he wrote, "Be anxious for nothing, but in everything by prayer and supplication, *with thanksgiving*, let your requests be made known to God" (Philippians 4:6, emphasis added). Thanksgiving is the antidote to worry. Instead of praying to God with doubt or discontentment, we can approach God in a spirit of thanksgiving. That's because God promised not to allow anything to happen to us that would be too much for us to bear (1 Corinthians 10:13).

Romans 8:28 establishes the overarching principle we need to keep in mind: "We know that all things work together for good to those who love God, to those who are the called according to His purpose." God's providence—which is His sovereign overruling and arranging of all of life's contingencies into a divine plan for the blessing of believers—should cause us to be thankful for anything that happens in our lives.

Because God actually uses all difficulties for our good, there is nothing we cannot thank Him for. Peter said that God will "perfect, establish, strengthen, and settle" us in the midst of our suffering (1 Peter 5:10). He also said we are to cast "all [our] care upon Him, for He cares for [us]" (1 Peter 5:7). In doing so, we express thankfulness for His providence, His promise of perfecting us, the glory He will receive from accomplishing His will, and for the promise of future blessings.

So be filled all the time with praise. In so doing, you'll find yourself released from fear and worry. Give every situation over to God's sovereign control, trusting Him because you know His history of wisdom and power and you understand His promise to supply all your needs (Philippians 4:19). Nothing about you escapes Him (Psalm 139:3). You know He cares about you (1 Peter 5:7), and He has the power to overcome every difficulty (Psalms 62:11). But He uses suffering to perfect you to be like Christ (Philippians 1:6), and His power and understanding are infinite (Psalm 147:5).

A PRAYER *of* CHARLES SPURGEON

O Thou blessed God! The joy of knowing that we are Thine forever, Thine in the trials of life, and Thine in the last dread of death, and then Thine in resurrection, Thine throughout eternity! We do therefore worship Thee, O God, not as a constraining nor under terror or pressure, but cheerfully and gladly, ascribing unto Thee praise, and power, and dominion, and glory, and honour, world without end.

We wish we knew how to do something for Thee. We pray that we may be helped to do so ere we die; yea, that every flying hour may confess that we have brought Thy Gospel some renown; that we may so live as to extend the Redeemer's kingdom at least in some little measure; that ours may not be a fruitless, wasted life; that no faculty of ours may lay by and rust; but to the utmost of our capacity may we be helped of the Divine Spirit to spend our whole life in real adoration.

We know that he prays that serves, he praises that gives, he adores that obeys, and the life is the best music. Oh! set it to good music, we pray Thee, and help us all through to keep to each note, and may there be no false note in all the singing of our life, but all be according to that sacred score which is written out so fully in the life music of our Lord.

A PRAYER *of* JOHN MACARTHUR

Our most holy God, we thank You for every opportunity to worship You. Remind us that such occasions will one day end and we will enter into heavenly praise—a heavenly praise that will never cease, joy that will never end, adoration that will continue forever where no flesh will grow weary, no congregation dispersed, no love wane, no affections diminish, no thoughts wander, no will weaken but all will be adoring praise forever and ever.

We thank You for each taste of that heaven to come. May our hearts truly grasp the glory of Your person, the wonder of Your goodness and grace. May our feeble prayers even show us the emptiness and vanity of our sins. Deepen in us the conviction that in our most fervent prayers, our most honest confessions we fall short—we are ever needing to repent.

By the Spirit give us abiding grace and insight that we might learn from You today, and may the seed sown take deep root and bring a full harvest. May all who see us take knowledge that we have been with You and that You have taught us our need as sinners, You have revealed to us a finished and glorious salvation. You have enriched us with all spiritual blessings. You have chosen us to show forth Jesus to all around us. Our great Creator, our mighty protector, our gracious preserver, we thank You for loading our lives with loving kindness, for making us Your purchased possession, for redeeming us from all guilt. We rejoice in all of this in the name of Jesus Christ.

CHAPTER SIX

PETITION

fter you have confessed your sin, praised and thanked God for who He is and what He has done, you are then ready to petition Him about matters on your heart.

Another word for petition that appears frequently in the Bible is "supplication." The root idea for the Greek word translated "supplication" meant "to bring an olive branch to a sovereign." If someone wanted a favor from a king, he would go before him, bow down, and offer him an olive branch as a symbol of peace. In a similar way, when we go to God with our requests, recognizing that He is ultimately the only One who can adequately deal with the issues of our hearts, we are in a sense offering an olive branch to Him.

God wants to hear what burdens us, and we do not need to be afraid to take those burdens to Him. We cast all our cares on the One who cares for us (1 Peter 5:7).

THE OBJECTS *of* OUR PETITIONS

God wants to hear what we desire. Philippians 4:6 invites us to tell him without timidity the desires of our hearts: "Be anxious for nothing, but in everything by prayer and supplication, with thanksgiving, let your requests be made known to God." We should not be anxious over adverse circumstances in our lives, because we can take them to our loving and infinitely rich heavenly Father.

Far more important than praying for ourselves is our need to offer petitions on behalf of others. Ephesians 6:18 says we are to be "praying always with all prayer and supplication ... for all the saints." But what do we typically pray about for others? If you are like most Christians, you pray about the issues your fellow believers tell you about. So you find your prayer list usually consisting of requests concerning someone's broken leg, someone's cardiac problems, or surgery for someone's relative. You might also have on your list a friend's need for a job, a car, or place to live. And it is important that, regarding such things, we support one another in prayer.

I am concerned, however, that the prayers of most saints rarely get beyond making petition for their own and others' physical needs, when we should be far more concerned about spiritual matters. The physical is unimportant by comparison. What really prompts me to petition the Lord is seeing another Christian who is not having victory over sin and is not experiencing God's best gifts in his life.

When I pray, I want to pray for the advancement of God's kingdom in the lives of His people. I pray for souls to be won to Christ. Believers are in a spiritual war, and we ought to be praying constantly for victory.

Believers are in a spiritual war,
and we ought to be praying constantly for victory.

Do you know the needs of the people around you? Are you aware of the spiritual needs of your spouse, children, parents, siblings, friends, neighbors, and the people in your Bible study? Do you pray for them? Unfortunately, we all tend to pray only when disaster strikes—perhaps some preventative praying would eliminate the need to pray so often for rescue.

Paul commands us to pray "for all the saints" (Ephesians 6:18). I personally have a commitment not to focus on myself as the subject of my petitioning. I do ask for the Lord's provision of my needs, but I mostly concentrate on praying for others' needs. I know I am already abundantly supported in prayer because others are praying for me. That is the way the Body of Christ grows in love.

Paul illustrates praying for others in two prayers recorded in his epistle to the Ephesians. They are examples of petitions that deal with the spiritual issues and battles we all face daily. Paul first prayed for believers' understanding of their spiritual resources in Christ; then he prayed they would know how to experience God's power in their lives.

A PETITION FOR *an* UNDERSTANDING
of SPIRITUAL RESOURCES

The first of these two example prayers is in Ephesians 1:15-23, where Paul prays that believers will understand their wonderful spiritual resources in Christ:

Therefore I also, after I heard of your faith in the Lord Jesus and your love for all the saints, do not cease to give thanks for you, making mention of you in my prayers: that the God of our Lord Jesus Christ, the Father of glory, may give to you the spirit of wisdom and revelation in the knowledge of Him, the eyes of your understanding being enlightened; that you may know what is the hope of His calling, what are the riches of the glory of His inheritance in the saints, and what is the exceeding greatness of His power toward us who believe, according to the working of His mighty power which He worked in Christ when He raised Him from the dead and seated Him at His right hand in the heavenly places, far above all principality and power and might and dominion, and every name that is named, not only in this age but also in that which is to come.

Paul wrote this letter from a prison cell in Rome. He had not been to the city of Ephesus for four years, but he maintained a genuine bond of love for the Ephesian believers. Paul particularly rejoiced concerning two things he had heard about the Ephesians: their faith in Jesus Christ and their love for one another (Ephesians 1:15-16).

The apostle's prayer then becomes a petition to God that the Ephesians might understand their privileges in Christ. It is vital that all Christians comprehend what their spiritual resources are, but apart from supernatural spiritual insight, even the most intellectual believer can't grasp the full range of spiritual privilege. That's why Paul prays for the Ephesians with these words: "that the God of our Lord Jesus Christ, the Father of glory, may give to you the spirit of wisdom and revelation in the knowledge of Him" (Ephesians 1:17).

The key word here is "spirit," which in the Greek normally means "wind," "breath," or "air." But it can also refer to attitude or disposition; so Paul is in essence asking God through the Holy Spirit to give the Ephesians wisdom and enlightenment (1 Corinthians 2:10-12).

"Wisdom" refers to the practical application of the truth revealed. Paul knew there is a wide difference between "knowledge of spiritual things" and "spiritual knowledge." It is one thing to know a lot of theology, but it is something quite beyond to have sufficient wisdom to apply that knowledge. Paul's prayer for the Ephesians and all believers is that they both know the deep truths of salvation and that they appreciate and apply them more and more. To assure that will happen, he wants all to know

- the greatness of God's plan,
- the greatness of His power,
- and the greatness of His Son.

THE GREATNESS *of* GOD'S PLAN

Understanding the truth begins when we see the greatness of the divine plan for us. Paul's petition seeks a divine grace from God that has "the eyes of your understanding . . . enlightened; that you may know what is the hope of His calling, what are the riches of the glory of His inheritance in the saints" (Ephesians 1:18). "The eyes of [our] understanding" denotes the thinking process of our inner person. Only the Spirit's intervention can unlock our spiritual understanding of God's glorious purpose.

> *Now we have received, not the spirit of the world, but the Spirit who is from God, that we might know the things that have been freely given to us by God.*
>
> — 1 CORINTHIANS 2:12

Even the best of human intellectual effort is terribly inadequate (1 Corinthians 2:14; 2 Corinthians 4:4, 6).

Paul wants us especially to apprehend two specific aspects of God's great plan: the hope of His calling and the riches of His inheritance. "Calling" refers to our election before the foundation of the world, and "hope" is our eternal glory with the Lord Jesus. Paul prays that believers will understand the amazing fact of God's choosing them in eternity past, His glory in eternity future, and all He has given us in between. "Hope" entails our assurance that God will do what He says concerning our salvation and sanctification (1 Thessalonians 5:24).

"Saints" (Ephesians 1:18) are all those who believe—the ones whom God has chosen for salvation and given a heavenly "inheritance." That inheritance includes all that the Lord has to give—endless spiritual riches for eternity. Later in the letter, Paul calls God's riches "unsearchable" (Ephesians 3:8), but that doesn't keep him from mentioning them here and several other places (Ephesians 1:7; 2:4; 3:16). Those riches are indeed more than sufficient for any circumstances we might face, and they are available simply by letting "the word of Christ dwell in you richly" (Colossians 3:16).

It is an immeasurable, incomprehensible blessing for us as believers to know the immense privilege of being in Christ. In fact, all God's riches are ours because we are part of His plan—that's why Paul prayed that we would have the joy of that understanding.

THE GREATNESS *of* GOD'S POWER

Paul describes the second reality he wants us to understand as "the exceeding greatness of His power toward us who believe, according to the working of His mighty power which He worked in Christ when He raised Him from the dead and seated Him at His right hand in the heavenly places" (Ephesians 1:19-20). "Power" comes from the Greek *dunamis*, which gives us our English word "dynamite."

Paul knew how the power of God worked in his own life and ministry, and he prayerfully desired that fellow believers realize the same benefit is available to them.

To further stress the dynamic quality of divine power, Paul says it is "working." That is again from a familiar Greek word (*energeia*), from which we get the English term "energy." The apostle prays that we would be energized by God's mighty power, the same power that created the universe and raised Jesus from the dead (Colossians 2:12).

Paul knew how the power of God worked in his own life and ministry (Colossians 1:28-29; 1 Thessalonians 1:5), and he prayerfully desired that fellow believers realize the same benefit is available to them (Philippians 3:10; 4:13).

THE GREATNESS *of* GOD'S SON

Paul in this model petition would also like his readers to know the greatness of Jesus Christ, which is "far above all principality and power and might and dominion, and every name that is named, not only in this age but also in that which is to come" (Ephesians 1:21).

The Father has elevated the Son far above all other beings, including angels, Satan, demons, and all unbelieving humanity who serve the powers of darkness. None is equal or superior to Him. Ephesians 1:21 is also a symbolic reference to the King elevated above His subjects—Christians who bow down and submit to His will. It is the picture of the Body of Christ, the church, of which Christ is the Head.

As we endeavor to serve the Lord, we need to remember Christ's divine presence in us (Colossians 1:15-18; 2:9) and His sympathetic understanding of us (Hebrews 4:15). So Paul prays that fellow Christians apprehend the spirit of wisdom and revelation as they experience the greatness of God's power and rely on the greatness of His Son—all of which is according to God's great eternal plan. That is an example of how we should pray for fellow Christians—for their grasp of the glories of redemptive theology. This is far more important than praying for earthly and physical problems.

A PETITION *for* THE RELEASE *of* GOD'S POWER

The second Pauline prayer worthy of following as we offer petitions for others is Ephesians 3:14-21.

For this reason I bow my knees to the Father of our Lord Jesus Christ, from whom the whole family in heaven and earth is named, that He would grant you, according to the riches of His glory, to be strengthened with might through His Spirit in the inner man, that Christ may dwell in your hearts through faith; that you, being rooted and grounded in love, may be able to comprehend with all the saints what is the width and length and depth and height—to know the love of Christ which passes knowledge; that you may be filled with all the fullness of God. Now to Him who is able to do exceedingly abundantly above all that we ask or think, according to the power that works in us, to Him be glory in the church by Christ Jesus to all generations, forever and ever. Amen.

This prayer outlines for us five aspects of divine power that are available to all Christians:
- Inner strength
- Indwelling of Christ
- Incomprehensible love
- Infinite fullness
- Immeasurable power

Paul bows his knees in prayer to God when he realizes the wealth of resources he and all believers, as members of God's family (Ephesians 2:18-19), have in His plan.

INNER STRENGTH

On the basis of that prayerful preface, Paul asks that God would strengthen the believers "in the inner man" (Ephesians 3:16). All who know Christ need inner strength to cope with the stress and pressures of everyday living, thus Paul prays that the Ephesians "be strengthened with might." That phrase literally means "empowered with power," which emphasizes the tremendous spiritual strength available to the believer's inner person. Such strength comes "through His Spirit," which simply means believers must be Spirit-filled, living in Spirit awareness, and submitting to the authority of the Holy Spirit in everything they think, say, and do. That filling and empowering by the Spirit occurs as we let the Word of Christ dwell in us richly (Colossians 3:16), pray, and submit to God's revealed will in our daily lives.

All who know Christ need inner strength to cope with the stress and pressures of everyday living.

Paul understood the principles of the Spirit-filled life and inner strength, even though they are often worked out in the midst of human weakness:

> And He said to me, "My grace is sufficient for you, for My strength is made perfect in weakness." Therefore most gladly I will rather boast in my infirmities that the power of Christ may rest upon me. Therefore I take

pleasure in infirmities, in reproaches, in needs, in persecutions, in distresses, for Christ's sake. For when I am weak, then I am strong.

— 2 C O R I N T H I A N S 1 2 : 9 - 1 0

Paul was not stressed out or spiritually defeated or depressed in his inner being over his own weakness. Instead he was strong because he depended on the Spirit to fill his life with divine power (Acts 20:24; 2 Corinthians 4:8-10, 16; 11:23-28). The apostle knew that being filled with—controlled by—the Holy Spirit is the first step for releasing God's power in the believer's inner life, thus he prays that his brethren will lay hold of that reality.

THE INDWELLING CHRIST

Paul's second petition (Ephesians 3:17) is that Christ would dwell in Christians' hearts. "Dwell" translates a Greek word that literally means "to settle down." In this context it connotes the already-present Christ becoming comfortable in a believer's heart. But this indwelling cannot happen if sin and disobedience are present. Only when the Lord controls every aspect of our lives can He really be at home in our hearts.

Paul prays that the Holy Spirit would lovingly cause the Ephesian believers to obey Him and thereby yield every part of their lives to Jesus Christ. In gracious condescension, our Lord is willing to make His home in our hearts. "If anyone loves Me, he will keep My word; and My Father will love him, and We will come to him and make Our home with him" (John 14:23). Jesus wants to "settle down" in the heart of every believer, and we should pray toward that end, not only for ourselves but also for our fellow Christians.

INCOMPREHENSIBLE LOVE

After Christ indwells the believer's heart, genuine love grows. Using the metaphor of the mature tree, Paul goes on to ask the believers to be "rooted and grounded in love" (Ephesians 3:17). When the world fails to recognize us as Christians, we are lacking in love for one another (John 13:34-35). But when we are spiritually strengthened inwardly by the Holy Spirit and Christ indwells us, our lives will radiate the incomprehensible love of the Lord Jesus. Thus Paul's petition says, "that you ... may be able to comprehend with all the saints what is the width and length and depth and height—to know the love of Christ which passes knowledge" (Ephesians 3:17-19). Before we can love other people—even other Christians—as we ought, we must not only be rooted and grounded in love, we must comprehend it.

In the Greek, "comprehend" means "to seize" something and make it your own. That's what Paul prays the Ephesians will do—take hold of the love of Christ in all its dimensions: "width and length and depth and height" (Ephesians 3:18). The first-century church used the cross to remind itself of these proportions of Christ's love. The post of the cross points upward and downward (height and depth); the crosspiece points to the horizons (breadth and length).

All believers need to have assurance about the dimensions of the Lord's love for us, especially in times of trial and tribulation. And every circumstance, easy or difficult, is an opportunity for us to display Christ's love. We should pray for a complete grasp of that love, on behalf of other Christians as well as ourselves.

INFINITE FULLNESS

The next aspect of divine power that Paul wants believers to experience is "all the fullness of God" (Ephesians 3:19). He petitions the Lord that they experience total spiritual richness. Paul is asking that the Ephesians would possess (as much as possible in the Spirit's power) the essential, undiminished characteristics of God. We can illustrate the concept this way. Suppose someone draws a thimble full of water from a lake. His thimble is essentially filled with the lake's water, yet the entire lake obviously does not fit into the thimble. The thimble contains the lake's basic "fullness"—representative particles of every lake water ingredient are present.

In a similar fashion, we as believers can possess God's fullness—His essential characteristics—without in any way diminishing who He is or becoming Him. We are thereby able to communicate godly love, wisdom, holiness, and graciousness to the world around us. Today we encounter too few Christians who consistently manifest the fullness of God. That's why we need to pray for His fullness in our life and the lives of believers we know. Christians communicate who God is not only by speaking the Scriptural truth, but also by displaying the essence of His character in their lives.

Every circumstance is an opportunity
for us to display Christ's love.

Finally, even beyond possessing the fullness of God, Paul prays for us to know how to unleash the divine power in us. The apostle's final petition begins, "Now to Him who is able to do exceedingly abundantly ... according to the power that works in us" (Ephesians 3:20). In another letter Paul in effect amplifies the concept of unleashing God's immeasurable power: "We have this treasure in earthen vessels, that the excellence of the power may be of God and not of us" (2 Corinthians 4:7). Only when we are aware of our own inadequacies and lack of power will we truly see God's power at work through us in serving the church and evangelizing the world. That is an awesome blessing to contemplate, and worthy of much prayer for others and ourselves in the Body of Christ.

At this point you might ask, "Why bother with all this stuff concerning petitions? My fellow Christians and I are going to heaven, even if we don't understand and experience all the truths of spiritual resources and God's power."

My answer to that is, "We bother because God wants to be glorified in His church now." "To Him be glory in the church by Christ Jesus to all generations, forever and ever. Amen" (Ephesians 3:21). We ought to be able to say "Amen" to that prayer and to Paul's other model prayer of petition in Ephesians 1:15-23. In that way we'll be affirming, "Let these realities be true in my life and in the lives of my fellow believers," so that the Lord may be honored in His church and before the watching world. This is essential to effective gospel witness.

Lord, look upon Thy people. We might pray about our troubles. We will not; we will only pray against our sins. We might come to Thee about our weariness, about our sickness, about our disappointment, about our poverty; but we will leave all that, we will only come about sin. Lord, make us holy, and then do what Thou wilt with us.

Lord, help the converted child to be correct in his relation to his parents; help the Christian father or mother to be right in dealing with children, "may they provoke not their children to anger, lest they may discourage" (Colossians 3:21, KJV). Take away willfulness from the young; take away impatience from the old. Lord help Christian men of business. May they act uprightly; and may Christian workpeople give to their masters that which is just and equal in the way of work in return for wage. May we as Christians be always standing upon our rights, but always be willing each one to minister to the help of others.

And, oh that as Christians we might be humble! Lord take away that stiff-necked, that proud look; take away from us the spirit of "stand by, for I am holier than thou"; make us condescend to men of low estate; ay, and even to men of low morals, low character. May we seek them out, seek their good. Oh! give to the church of Christ an intense love for the souls of men. May it make our hearts break to think that they will perish in their sin. May we grieve every day because of the sin of this City. Set a mark upon our forehead and let us be known to Thyself as men that sigh and cry for all the abominations that are done in the midst of the City.

A PRAYER *of* JOHN MACARTHUR

Father, the psalmist has given testimony to Your mercy and confessed his faith and heard the response that Your eyes are on the faithful. Those You will bless who demonstrate that they belong to You through faith by a righteous life and the wicked shall be destroyed. This is the age-old message that those who come before You through faith receive mercy, are given the power to live to please You. Those who have no such power because they do not come and embrace Your salvation shall receive only Your judgment.

We thank You, Father, that You have been gracious to us and so we sing of Your mercy, we sing praises to You. Our faith is in You, our expectation is from You. Our love goes out toward You. We believe You. We submit to Your Word. We are eager to do Your will. We trust in Your promises. We rest on Your providence. We thank You that the court of conscience affirms that we are Yours through the witness of the Spirit. We thank You that we do not need signs and wonders to believe, for Your Word is more sure. We have cast our anchor in the port of peace, knowing that we are secure in the present and the future from all the storms that rage because we're held in the nail-pierced hands of Jesus Christ.

We acknowledge, O God, that You are good and wise and just and holy and merciful. You are the fountain, the source of all law. You're also the fountain and source of all grace to those who having broke Your law come to You for forgiveness. We yield to Your sovereignty, wanting only what You want for us. We ask that You would grant us silence in our heart in place of murmuring and complaining.

May our truest wishes be those things that advance the Kingdom and not our own will. May we never find fault with Your providences. May we only look for Your mercy in them all knowing that trouble draws us to You and that's where we need to be for joy and blessing. When we sin and are rebellious, help us to repent, take away our mourning and give out music. Remove our sackcloth and adorn us with the garments of joy. Take away our sighing, fill our mouths with song. And when we are restored and rest again in You and walk in the light of Your truth, may we know the fullness of Your blessing. These things we ask in the name of Jesus Christ.

CHAPTER SEVEN

HINDRANCES OF PRAYER

I f you are like most believers, you find that prayer, in spite of its amazing, blessed benefits, is a difficult spiritual duty to fulfill. That is likely one of the main reasons you are reading this book. D. A. Carson readily acknowledges the reality of prayer's difficulty in the preface to his book *A Call to Spiritual Reformation*: "I doubt if there is any Christian who has not sometimes found it difficult to pray. In itself this is neither surprising nor depressing: it is not surprising, because we are still pilgrims with many lessons to learn; it is not depressing, because struggling with such matters is part of the way we learn" (Grand Rapids: Baker, 1992, 9).

Of course, there are some important reasons why prayer is so often difficult for us—what we might call hindrances to prayer. The main hindrance is the general presence of sin. Psalm 66:18 says, "If I regard iniquity in my heart, the Lord will not hear." Sin builds a barrier to prayer (Isaiah 59:2). If we look carefully at our lives, we can probably identify some specific sins that hinder our prayer lives, or at times keep us from prayer altogether.

The most common hindrances to our prayers are:
- *Carnality and unconcern*
- *An unforgiving spirit*
- *Strife at home*
- *Doubt*

CARNALITY *and* UNCONCERN

The flesh is a serious hindrance to prayer and to other disciplines of the Christian life because it is characterized by all sorts of sinful behaviors and attitudes. When we received our new nature at conversion, our old sinful nature, the flesh, remained. It will be with us until we are glorified (Romans 8:18-25), and will continually seek to hinder and oppose our new nature.

No Christian is exempt from struggling with the flesh, not even Paul:

> *For what I am doing, I do not understand. For what I will to do, that I do not practice; but what I hate, that I do ... For the good that I will to do, I do not do; but the evil I will not to do, that I practice ... For I delight in the law of God according to the inward man. But I see another law in my members, warring against the law of my mind, and bringing me into captivity to the law of sin which is in my members.*

— ROMANS 7:15, 19, 22-23

When we were born anew, God imputed to us Christ's payment for sin's penalty (I Peter 3:18) and removed sin's controlling power (Romans 6:5-7; Galatians 2:19-20), but the tendency to evil remains within us. One word that best characterizes our flesh is "selfishness," the tendency to focus on our own will and interests and against God's. That has been the center of sin ever since the fall of Adam and Eve, and such self-centeredness easily hinders us from praying as we ought.

The object of prayer should not be to selfishly ask God for things without regard for how such requests might dishonor His name or defy His purposes. In fact, Scripture says God will not give us what we selfishly desire: "You ask and do not receive, because you ask amiss, that you may spend it on your pleasures" (James 4:3). Instead, we must always pray as Jesus did when He told the Father, "Nevertheless not My will, but Yours, be done" (Luke 22:42). As Jesus taught us to pray, so we say, "Your will be done on earth, as it is in heaven" (Matthew 6:10).

Our carnal selfishness can also hinder our prayer life because it tends to make us totally unconcerned about the needs of others. This hindrance to prayer can stem from our failure to heed Paul's admonition:

> *Let nothing be done through selfish ambition or conceit,*
> *but in lowliness of mind let each esteem others better*
> *than himself. Let each of you look out not only for his*
> *own interests, but also for the interests of others.*

PHILIPPIANS 2:3-4

Proverbs 21:13 says, "Whoever shuts his ears to the cry of the poor will also cry himself and not be heard."

The principle is simply this: If you lack concern for others, God will be indifferent to your needs. Before you go to the Lord in prayer, make sure you are not being indifferent to the needs of others, or praying for yourself as if you were isolated from the rest of God's people.

An Unforgiving Spirit

An unwillingness to forgive others is another specific sin that can hinder prayer. Jesus said, "Whenever you stand praying, if you have anything against anyone, forgive him, that your Father in heaven may also forgive you your trespasses" (Mark 11:25). This is a prerequisite to prayer—before God will hear your prayers, you need to forgive anyone who has offended you.

Matthew 5:23-24 offers a prescription for meeting that prerequisite:

> *"If you bring your gift to the altar, and there remember that your brother has something against you, leave your gift there before the altar; and go your way. First be reconciled to your brother, and then come and offer your gift."*

The scene described was a familiar one to the Jews. It probably depicted the Day of Atonement when worshipers brought animals to the priests to sacrifice for the people's sins. But the person was not to make his offering if he remembered some unresolved conflict with another Israelite—reconciliation with his brother was the first priority.

We cannot truly worship God or expect Him to answer our prayers if we harbor resentment or bitterness for someone. How can we ask God to pour out all of His love, mercy, and grace on us—undeserving sinners—if we won't forgive and be reconciled to another undeserving sinner?

The phrase "your brother has something against you" could also refer to some anger or hatred he has toward you. You should do everything you can to seek his forgiveness and reconcile. Obviously only God can change someone's heart or attitude, but we should do as much as humanly possible to seek reconciliation before we pray. We cannot righteously ask God for forgiveness when we haven't granted pardon to a fellow believer.

In Matthew 18:23-35 Jesus told a parable of a king who called his servants (probably regional governors) together to settle accounts with them. The king discovered that one of the servants owed him a vast fortune. But when the servant pleaded with him and promised to pay back the king all that he owed, the king forgave the servant the entire debt. But this servant immediately left the gracious king's presence and demanded repayment from someone who owed him much less. When he didn't get it, this unjust servant had that man thrown into prison. And the king retaliated.

When we are unforgiving, we render our prayers of confession ineffective and cut ourselves off from the forgiveness God would grant us for our sins (Matthew 6:14-15). When we refuse to forgive we also forfeit the inner peace, spiritual power, and spiritual growth that the Lord would otherwise grant through our prayers. So make this your objective: before you ask God to be gracious to you, do some self-examination to make sure you are treating others with the same kind of gracious, forgiving favor you want to receive from God.

STRIFE *at* HOME

Another potential hindrance to prayer is discord in the home, or conflict in family relationships, especially between husbands and wives. Peter specifically named this as a hindrance to prayer and said husbands ought to be sure they have a God-honoring relationship with their wives so their prayers will not go unanswered: "Husbands, likewise dwell with them with understanding, giving honor to the wife, as to the weaker vessel, and as being heirs together of the grace of life, that your prayers may not be hindered" (1 Peter 3:7). In context, this verse concludes Peter's admonition to wives and husbands who may have unsaved spouses, but his exhortation also has a wider application.

What should be the attitude of the Christian husband to guarantee answered prayer? Peter mentions three things.

First, the husband should be considerate of his wife's needs and be sensitive to her feelings. The Greek word for "dwell" means to live with someone in a close, intimate way. The Septuagint (Greek Old Testament) uses this term to mean sexual intercourse. "Understanding" comes from the word that means deep, experiential knowledge. So husbands are to live with their wives in a deeply intimate and respectful manner, being sensitive to their deepest physical and emotional needs (Ephesians 5:25-29).

Second, the husband ought to demonstrate chivalry in the home. He should remember his own weakness and realize that his wife is physically weaker ("the weaker vessel"). So husbands should protect, provide for, nourish, and cherish their wives.

Third, husbands must keep in mind that they and their wives are true companions—"heirs together of the grace of life." That simply means married couples should appreciate their status, realizing it is one of the best earthly gifts life offers. They are to nurture their relationship through meaningful friendship, fellowship, and partnership in all of life's important matters.

When there is a serious conflict in relationships and the head of the home is not demonstrating the attitudes Peter mentions, his prayer communication with God will be severely hindered, perhaps even closed.

DOUBT

Finally, doubt can be a major hindrance to prayer. James 1:6-7, in regard to a believer's asking the Lord for wisdom—or anything else—says:

> But let him ask in faith, with no doubting, for he who doubts is like a wave of the sea driven and tossed by the wind. For let not that man suppose that he will receive anything from the Lord.

God requires the right kind of asking when we come to Him in prayer. We must ask without doubting, which means our prayers have to be accompanied by authentic trust in God's character, purposes, and promises.

Yet some believers doubt God's power, concern, or provision. They might think they are undeserving or that their needs are unworthy of God's attention. In abstract, both of those thoughts are true, but they are also irrelevant because God sovereignly chooses to take great interest in the smallest, most insignificant matters in His children's lives. Other Christians dispute with God and ask why they are having difficulties or why He doesn't send them immediate solutions to their problems.

But prayer that doesn't trust the Lord's promises, or doubts that He is trustworthy or able, is a terrible affront to God. Instead of harboring such doubts, you need to remember that "without faith it is impossible to please Him, for he who comes to God must believe that He is, and that He is a rewarder of those who diligently seek Him" (Hebrews 11:6).

The power of the sinful flesh, a spirit of unforgiveness, domestic strife, an attitude of doubt—all these, though not the only sins to do so, are significant hindrances to prayer. Fortunately you can deal with all of them at once, which is the first thing we ought to do in the presence of God: confess our sins (1 John 1:9). Once we have done that, we can enjoy a clear channel of communication with the Lord, go on to praise Him, make our requests known to Him, and benefit from unhindered fellowship with Him.

Prayer that doesn't trust the Lord's
promises is a terrible affront to God

O Lord, many of us feel like the lame man at the Beautiful Gate of the temple. Come by this way and make the lame ones perfectly sound. O Lord, Thou canst do by Thy servants to-day what Thou didst by them in the olden time. Work miracles of mercy even upon outer court worshippers who are too lame to get into the holy place.

But there are many who feel like that man when he was restored. We would follow our Restorer, the Prince of Life, into the temple, leaping and walking and praising God. He has gone into the temple in the highest sense, up to the throne of God. He climbs, and we would follow, up the steps of the temple one by one, made meet. We would come nearer and nearer to the throne of God.

Draw us nearer, Lord, draw us into the inner Sanctuary; draw us within the place which once was hidden by the veil which Christ has rent; bring us right up to the throne of grace, and there beholding the glory of God above the Mercy Seat may we have communion with the Most High. Heal all our diseases and forgive us all our trespasses.

Still, Lord, though healed of a former lameness so that now we have strength, we need a further touch from Thee; we are so apt to get dull and stupid; come and help us, Lord Jesus. A vision of Thy face will brighten us; but to feel Thy Spirit touching us will make us vigorous. Oh! for the leaping and the walking of the man born lame. May we to-day dance with holy joy like David before the Ark of God. May a holy exhilaration take possession of every part of us; may we be glad in the Lord; may our mouth be filled with laughter, and our tongue with singing, "for the LORD hath done great things for us whereof we are glad" (Psalm 126:3, KJV).

To-day help Thy people to put on Christ. May we live as those who are alive from the dead, for He is the quickening Spirit; and may we feel Him to be so. If any part of us still dead, Lord, quicken it. May the life which has taken possession of our heart take possession of our head; may the brain be active in holy thought; may our entire being, indeed, respond to the life of Christ, and may we live in newness of life.

We would fain fall down on our faces and worship the Son of God to-day. It is such a wonder that He should have loved us; and He has done such wonderful things for us and in us that we may still call Him God's unspeakable gift. He is unspeakably precious to our souls.

Lord, send Thy life throughout the entire Church. Lord, visit Thy church, restore sound doctrine, restore holy and earnest living. Take away from professors their apparent love for frivolities, their attempts to meet the world on its own ground, and give back the old love to the doctrines of the cross, the doctrines of the Christ of God; and once more may free grace and dying love be the music that shall refresh the church, and make her heart exceeding glad.

CHAPTER EIGHT

MOTIVATIONS
TO PRAYER

 ow devoted are you to prayer? Do you pray as
often and for as many things as you ought? If
you are like most of us, you will answer with a
definite "No."

Even as a pastor, I continually find myself feeling dissatisfied
with my prayer life—I often feel that I simply have not prayed
as much as I should and partly because I am overwhelmed with
more people and prayer requests than it is humanly possible to
intercede for. My burden to have a better prayer life constantly

causes me to examine my motivation and ask, "Is something lacking in my spiritual life? Am I really motivated to pray if I don't pray as I should?" Every Christian ought to ask such questions, and Scripture gives us plenty of motivations to overcome our lack of prayer.

David tells us:

> *Delight yourself also in the* LORD, *and He shall give you the desires of your heart.*
>
> — PSALM 37:4

Jesus instructed His disciples:

> *"So I say to you, ask, and it will be given to you; seek, and you will find; knock, and it will be opened to you. For everyone who asks receives, and he who seeks finds, and to him who knocks it will be opened."*
>
> — LUKE 11:9-10

John assures us:

> *Now this is the confidence that we have in Him, that if we ask anything according to His will, He hears us. And if we know that He hears us, whatever we ask, we know that we have the petitions that we have asked of Him.*
>
> — 1 JOHN 5:14-15

Those are wonderful promises, but if taken in isolation and not understood properly, someone might see them as rather selfish motivations; in other words, that the only reason we ought to pray is to fulfill our personal "wish list." But God's Word contains motivations to prayer that rise far above that, and I would like to challenge and encourage you in your prayer life by briefly discussing ten such motivations that will summarize what I have already written.

10 MOTIVATIONS *to* PRAY

1. Desire for the Lord's glory
2. Desire for fellowship with God
3. Desire for needs to be met
4. Desire for wisdom
5. Desire for deliverance from trouble
6. Desire for relief from fear and worry
7. Desire to offer thanks for past blessings
8. Desire to be free from the guilt of sin
9. Desire for the salvation of the lost
10. Desire for the spiritual growth of other believers

A Desire *for* the Lord's Glory

Our desire for the Lord's glory should be the first and foremost motivation for prayer. Daniel's model (Daniel 9:4-19) resulted from his longing for God's glory. The prophet prayed that God would cleanse His sinful people and restore them according to His purposes. Notice how he concludes his prayer:

> "O my God, incline Your ear and hear; open Your eyes and see our desolations, and the city which is called by Your name; for we do not present our supplications before You because of our righteous deeds, but because of Your great mercies. O Lord, hear! O Lord, forgive! O Lord, listen and act! Do not delay for your own sake, my God, for Your city and Your people are called by Your name."
>
> — Daniel 9:18-19

Our Lord echoed those sentiments in the opening sentences of His model prayer: "Our Father in heaven, hallowed be Your name. Your kingdom come. Your will be done on earth as it is in heaven" (Matthew 6:9-10). When we pray for God to be exalted, that His plan and promises be fulfilled, we are not praying for self; we are praying for Him, because we desire that the Lord be glorified.

A Desire *for* Fellowship *with* God

Another motivation to prayer stems from a genuine longing to be in the presence of God. That longing often begins when our heart feels lonely, estranged, or cut off from the Lord and therefore cries out for fellowship with Him. The psalmist so beautifully expresses this truth many times:

> *As the deer pants for the water brooks, so pants my soul for You, O God. My soul thirsts for God, for the living God. When shall I come and appear before God?*
>
> — PSALM 42:1-2

> *O God, You are my God; early will I seek You; my soul thirsts for You; my flesh longs for You ... So I have looked for You in the sanctuary, to see Your power and glory.*
>
> — PSALM 63:1-2

> *How lovely is Your tabernacle, O LORD of hosts! My soul longs, yes, even faints, for the courts of the LORD; my heart and my flesh cry out for the living God.*
>
> — PSALM 84:1-2

Furthermore, Psalm 27:1, 4 gives us powerful reasons for having such strong motivation to fellowship with God. David writes: *The LORD is my light and my salvation; whom shall I fear? The LORD is the strength of my life; of whom shall I be afraid? ... One thing I have desired of the LORD, that will I seek: that I may dwell in the house of the LORD all the days of my life, to behold the beauty of the LORD, and to inquire in His temple.*

A DESIRE *for*
NEEDS *to* BE MET

Christians should also be motivated to pray because they desire the Father to answer the concerns of their hearts with power and blessing. Jesus' guideline here ought to encourage us: "Give us this day our daily bread" (Matthew 6:11). It is right for us to ask God to supply the basics of daily life, although in affluent Western cultures, that prompter to prayer may be much harder to appreciate. But for many brothers and sisters in needy places across the world, such praying for the daily necessities of food, clothing, and shelter is a normal and natural way of life.

We should never presume that, just because God has so often graciously provided our daily needs without our asking, we can be indifferent to Him some day, for some purpose, allowing those needs to remain unmet for a while. We need to pray for our needs every day, even if it's simply to thank God for so mercifully supplying them when we don't deserve anything. But He promises to meet them only when we seek first His Kingdom and righteousness (Matthew 6:33).

We need to pray for our needs every day,
even if it's simply to thank God for so mercifully
supplying them when we don't deserve anything.

A Desire *for* Wisdom

James has this to say about the Christian's desire to obtain wisdom:

> *If any of you lacks wisdom, let him ask of God, who gives to all*
> *liberally and without reproach, and it will be given to him.*

— JAMES 1:5

If you believe that you don't need divine wisdom as you live in a sinful world, you're really deceived. When Jesus taught us to pray, He said, "Do not lead us into temptation, but deliver us from the evil one" (Matthew 6:13). That is a prayer for spiritual discernment, or spiritual wisdom.

We should be motivated constantly to pray something along these lines:

> *"Lord, please by Your Spirit give me the ability to*
> *discern when I am being led into something that is*
> *evil. Please give me the wisdom, insight, and scrip-*
> *tural sensitivity to allow me not to fall into the*
> *traps of the world, the flesh, or the devil."*

A DESIRE *for* DELIVERANCE *from* TROUBLE

Psalm 9:9 summarizes well the reason we ought to pray during times of trouble: "The LORD also will be a refuge for the oppressed, a refuge in times of trouble." This reassurance is reiterated many times in passages such as Psalm 18:6, 20:1, 27:5, 32:7, 46:1, and 106:44.

Sometimes the greater the trouble and distress we find ourselves in, the more we have failed to follow the other motivations to prayer. But periods of great difficulty tend to prompt us to unceasing prayer as we realize there is no human way of deliverance from our dilemma. The situation is reminiscent of the disobedient Jonah.:

> *Then Jonah prayed to the LORD his God from the fish's belly. And he said: "I cried out to the LORD because of my affliction, and He answered me. Out of the belly of Sheol I cried, and You heard my voice."*
>
> — JONAH 2:1-2

In the same fashion we also sometimes need to cry out to the Lord for deliverance.

A Desire for Relief from Fear and Worry

All believers can identify with the desire for relief from fear. If you're in distress and experiencing fear, worry, anxiety, and depression, what should you do? If you want a solution based on human wisdom, consult someone who does not rely on Scripture. But if you want a solution based on divine wisdom, the formula is simple. Just go to the Lord in persistent, continual prayer and you will experience His peace and find the right answers to all your questions and problems. As the apostle Paul told the Philippians:

> *Be anxious for nothing, but in everything by prayer*
> *and supplication, with thanksgiving, let your requests*
> *be made known to God; and the peace of God, which*
> *surpasses all understanding, will guard your hearts*
> *and minds through Christ Jesus.*

— PHILIPPIANS 4:6-7

Why do we ever want to go to other sources for answers to our anxieties when God has promised that relief from fear and worry is ours through prayer? We need the confidence of the psalmist, who wrote, "Hear me when I call, O God of my righteousness! You have relieved me in my distress; have mercy on me, and hear my prayer" (Psalm 4:1).

A DESIRE *to* OFFER
THANKS *for* PAST BLESSING

If we have a thankful heart and remember all that the Lord, in
His goodness, has done for us in the past, that ought to motivate
us to pray and at least offer God a simple thanks. The psalmist
provides an excellent example of remembering past blessings:

> *We have heard with our ears, O God, our fathers
> have told us, the deeds You did in their days, in days
> of old: You drove out the nations with Your hand, but
> them You planted; You afflicted the peoples, and cast
> them out. For they did not gain possession of the land
> by their own sword, nor did their own arm save them;
> but it was Your right hand, Your arm, and the light
> of Your countenance, because You favored them. You
> are my King, O God.*

> — PSALM 44:1-4

If I am really grateful for what God has done for me and for
others, it will motivate me to pray, as Paul prayed for the
believers:

> *We give thanks to God always for you all, making
> mention of you in our prayers, remembering without
> ceasing your work of faith, labor of love, and patience
> of hope in our Lord Jesus Christ in the sight of our
> God and Father*

> — 1 THESSALONIANS 1:2-3

A DESIRE *to* BE FREE *from* THE GUILT *of* SIN

Along with Psalm 51, Psalm 32 is a classic psalm that addresses the penitent believer's desire to be freed from sin's guilt. David expresses the matter well in the opening verses:

> Blessed is he whose transgression is forgiven, whose sin is covered. Blessed is the man to whom the LORD does not impute iniquity, and in whose spirit there is no deceit. When I kept silent, my bones grew old through my groaning all the day long. For day and night Your hand was heavy upon me; my vitality was turned into the drought of summer. I acknowledged my sin to You, and my iniquity I have not hidden. I said, "I will confess my transgressions to the LORD," and You forgave the iniquity of my sin.
>
> — PSALM 32:1-5

David opened up and confessed his sin to God. The deceit and cover-up was finished, and his psychosomatic ailments resulting from guilt were alleviated—because now he was forgiven and blessed. And the desires that motivated David ought to prompt us to incessant, penitential confession so that we also remain free from the guilt of unconfessed sin, and have the joy of salvation.

A DESIRE *for* THE
SALVATION *of* THE LOST

When you're compassionately concerned about lost people, you will be moved to pray for their salvation. The lost are all around us, and if you care about their souls you will have a persistent attitude of prayer for them as they cross your path and as their names come to your mind. We are instructed about this:

> *Therefore I exhort first of all that supplications, prayers, intercessions, and giving of thanks be made for all men, for kings and all who are in authority, that we may lead a quiet and peaceable life in all godliness and reverence. For this is good and acceptable in the sight of God our Savior, who desires all men to be saved and to come to the knowledge of the truth.*
>
> — 1 TIMOTHY 2:1-4

> *Brethren, my heart's desire and prayer to God for Israel is that they may be saved.*
>
> — ROMANS 10:1

> *The Lord is ... not willing that any should perish but that all should come to repentance.*
>
> — 2 PETER 3:9

If we don't pray unceasingly for the lost, then something is lacking concerning our compassion for them and we need to ask God to give us a new desire to pray for the unsaved.

A Desire *for* the Spiritual Growth *of* Other Believers

In his epistles the apostle Paul was a model in praying for others' spiritual growth. Such intercession is part of his New Testament letters, as we examined in Ephesians 1:15-19 and Ephesians 3:14-21.

Another powerful example of Paul's praying for spiritual growth is found in Colossians 1:9-12:

> *For this reason we also, since the day we heard it, do not cease to pray for you, and to ask that you may be filled with the knowledge of His will in all wisdom and spiritual understanding; that you may walk worthy of the Lord, fully pleasing Him, being fruitful in every good work and increasing in the knowledge of God; strengthened with all might, according to His glorious power, for all patience and longsuffering with joy; giving thanks to the Father who has qualified us to be partakers of the inheritance of the saints in the light.*

We often take for granted that fellow Christians will increase in their knowledge of the Lord. But He wants us to make that increase an object of regular prayer.

THE KEY *to* PRAYER MOTIVATION

If we are not following the mandate to "pray without ceasing" (1 Thessalonians 5:17), something is wrong with our desire to pray, something is missing at the motivational level. If that is true, how can we improve that situation? Let me share some things I've learned in my years of experience as a Christian.

The Lord by His Spirit taught me years ago that the only sure way to prompt and sustain a quality prayer life is to maintain a regular and disciplined study of the Word of God. As I, like Daniel (see Daniel 7:1–10:9), see His Word unfold His marvelous plan of redemption and the plan for His future glory, I begin to long for God's glorification (Revelation 22:20). As I see the glorious plan of God outlined in Scripture, I become consumed with His kingdom and His glory, which prompts me to pray more fervently for them.

The only sure way to prompt and sustain a quality prayer life is to maintain a regular and disciplined study of the Word of God.

The more I find God's person, character, and majesty revealed on the pages of Scripture (Isaiah 6:1-5; Revelation 5:8-14), the more I want to fellowship with Him through prayer. And the more I study the Bible and discover how God wants to provide everything to meet all the needs of His children (Psalm 145:17-19; Philippians 4:19), the more I'm prompted to pray to that end.

One of those most important needs is for wisdom and discernment, and God's Word is the perfect source for the insight and understanding we need to live in this difficult world.

> *God's Word is the perfect source for the insight and understanding we need to live in this difficult world.*

As I read how the Bible chronicles the many times through the centuries that God delivered His people from their troubles—

- *how He delivered His special servants from fear and worry (Elijah in 1 Kings 19:4-18)*
- *how some could praise Him as they were about to be tossed into a white-hot furnace (Shadrach, Meshach, and Abed-Nego in Daniel 3)*
- *how He delivered people from imprisonment (Joseph in Genesis 41:9-16; Peter in Acts 12:1-19; Paul and Silas in Acts 16:16-36)*

—as they trusted in Him, it reassures me to know that He will also deliver me from all kinds of cares and troubles as I lean on Him (1 Peter 5:6-7). The more I read and study the biblical record of all the events, blessings, and glories of redemptive history, the more it causes me to give thanks for what God has done.

Whenever I read again of the Lord's perfect plan of atonement (Genesis 3:15; Galatians 4:4-5), how He accomplished it through the death and resurrection of Christ (1 Corinthians 15:3-4), how He applied it to me by grace through faith (Ephesians 2:8-9), and how it gives me access to complete cleansing and forgiveness (Hebrews 10:19-23), it causes me to regularly confess my sins to God (1 John 1:9). And as I see how it grieves God and His Son when people refuse to turn to Him (Matthew 23:37-39; Ezekiel 18:23), it makes me prayerfully desire the salvation of the lost.

Whenever I see how from beginning to end the Word of God reveals His heart for His children to grow spiritually, that they should live in obedience and holiness, it reminds me to pray for the sanctification of fellow believers.

I firmly believe the foundational element to prompting a persistent, consistent prayer life is a faithful and disciplined plan to read, study, and meditate on the Word of God. Rarely do I come away from time spent in the Word without, in some way or another, being newly motivated and committed to praying more frequently and faithfully than I had before. The apostle Paul admonished us to "pray without ceasing," and that should be our way of life. Start today!

A PRAYER *of*
CHARLES SPURGEON

O God our Father, we do remember well when we were called to Thee; with many sweet and wooing voices we were bidden to return. Thou didst Thyself hang out the lights of mercy that we might know the way home, and Thy dear Son Himself came down to seek us. But we wandered still. It brings the tears to our eyes to think that we should have been so foolish and so wicked, for we often extinguished the light within and conscience we tried to harden, and we sinned against light and knowledge with a high hand against our God.

O happy day that sealed our pardon with the precious blood of Jesus, accepted by faith. We would recall the memory of that blessed season by repeating it. We come again now to the cross whereon the Saviour bled; we give another look of faith to Him. We trust we never take away our eyes off Him, but if we have done so we would look anew; we would gaze into the body of the Son of God, pierced with nails, parched with thirst, bleeding, dying, because "it pleased the Father to bruise Him; He hath put Him to grief" (Isaiah 53:10, KJV).

Lord God, we see in Thy crucified Son a sacrifice for sin; we see how Thou hast made Him to be sin for us that we might be made the righteousness of God in Him; and we do over again accept

Him to be everything to us. This is the victim by whose blood the covenant is made through faith; this is that paschal Lamb by the sprinkling of whose blood all Israel is secured; for Thou hast said, "When I see the blood I will pass over you" (Exodus 12:13, KJV). This is the blood which gives us access into that which is within the veil; this is the blood which now to our souls is drink indeed, and we do rejoice in the joy which this new wine of the covenant hath given unto our spirits.

We are not our own; we are bought with a price. Lord Jesus, renew Thy grasp of us, take us over again, for we do even with greater alacrity than ever before surrender ourselves to Thee, and so "bind the sacrifice with cords, even with cords to the horns of the altar" (Psalm 118:27, KJV). O Lord, I am Thy servant, and the son of Thine handmaid. Thou hast loosed my bonds. The Lord liveth, and blessed be my Rock. Henceforth within that Rock I hide myself. For Him I live. The Lord enable all His people with sincere hearts, with undivided hearts, thus again to give themselves up to Jesus, and do Thou set in them anew the marks and tokens of Thy possession till every one of us shall say as many of us can say, "From henceforth let no man trouble me; for I bear in my body the marks of the Lord Jesus Christ" (Galatians 6:17, KJV).

A Prayer *of* John MacArthur

It's little wonder, our God, that the Book of Psalms ends with rejoicing and joy because it rehearses Your eternal mercies, Your eternal faithfulness to Your covenant promise. It rehearses the fact that there's no one like You, that You are the Creator, the Sustainer of Your people. You are strong and mighty. You are righteous and just. Mercy and truth come from You.

And so we rejoice because Jesus Christ has made You our God, and we are Your people, and all Your ways of mercy end in our delight. Even Jesus Christ wept and sorrowed and suffered that we might rejoice. And then He sent us the Comforter that He might give us of His fruit love and joy, joy that comes because of the multiplying of Your promises, because of the guarantee of our future glory. Joy that comes because the Spirit is in us, a river of water gushing forth.

I thank You, O God, that You are preparing joy for us and us for eternal joy. We long for that joy. We wait for that eternal joy. And yet even in time You have measured out to us the richness of blessing that results in our joy even in this life. Though we may weep at night, always joy comes in the morning. Joy because we rest in Your love, joy because of pardon from sin, joy because of our title to heaven, joy because of our anticipated future unspotted state in glory, joy because we are unworthy recipients of Your grace. Joy because even though we fail in obedience and though we fail to worship You as we should, You forgive us.

In repentance we can draw water from the wells of forgiveness that brings us joy. And while our hearts reach out toward that eternal rest, where the work of redemption, sanctification, and preservation end in glory, though we look for that time of finished and perfect joy, though there is no joy like the joy of heaven, yet as long as we are here we thank You for the joy that is measured to us because all this great hope is secured in Christ. We thank You in His great name.

MY PERSONAL PRAYER

Reading about prayer is good, but your participation in prayer is what God wants. Let the guidance below help you remember the lessons of this book and apply them to your growing, vital prayer life. This is not a formula for all your prayers, but rather a simple tool to help you get started today.

Before you begin your prayer, search your heart. Are there unresolved issues that would hinder your prayers? Do you need to forgive someone? Do you doubt God? Is there strife at home? Is your carnal nature ruling you, or is your love of God in charge? (Chapter 7) Then as you pray, remember to ask in Christ's name and character. Ask in faith and Spirit, and ask from a pure heart. (Chapter 2)

Pray for God's glory. Praise Him. Acknowledge who He is.
(Chapters 2 & 5; Psalm 27; Psalm 84; Psalm 86; Habakkuk 3)

_____

_____

_____

_____

_____

_____

Confess to Him. (Chapter 4; Psalm 51; Daniel 9:4–19; 1 John 1:9)

_____

_____

_____

_____

_____

_____

_____

_____

_____

_____

_____

_____

_____

_____

_____

Pray about yourself and others. Thank Him for His mercy, goodness, and blessings. Ask Him for what you and others need—salvation, daily bread, forgiveness, guidance, deliverance, understanding of spiritual resources, and for the release of God's power. (Chapters 3 & 6; Psalm 44; Luke 11:5–10; Luke 18:2–5; Ephesians 1:15–23; Ephesians 3:14–21).

_____

_____

_____

_____

_____

_____

Pray again for God's glory. Pray that everything will be according to His will. Acknowledge your trust in Him. (Chapter 8, 1 John 5:14–15)

_____

_____

_____

_____

Now that you've prayed, don't forget this: Prayer must be an essential part of your life. It is your lifeline to God. It is your spiritual breath. Inhale the Word and the Spirit, and exhale God's glory. (Chapter 3)

FOR MORE INFORMATION

Grace to You is the Bible-teaching media ministry of John MacArthur. In addition to producing the world-wide Grace to You and Grace to You Weekend radio broadcasts, we distribute more than two dozen books by John MacArthur and have produced more than thirteen million audiocassette lessons since 1969. For more details about John MacArthur and all his Bible-teaching resources, contact us at 800-55-GRACE or www.gty.org.